THE HOW AND WHY WONDER BOOK OF

THE MOON

Written by
FELIX SUTTON

with additional material by
ALVIN MAURER and
OSCAR WEIGLE

Illustrated by

PLUTO

NEPTUNE · · MOONS

URANUS · · · · · MOONS

SATURN · · · · · · MOONS

JUPITER · · · · · · · MOONS

MARS · · MOONS

EARTH · MOON

VENUS

MERCURY

SUN

& DUNLAP
• NEW YORK

Introduction

The moon has been the subject of speculation and imaginative questioning by mankind through the ages. A close neighbor in space, its rhythmic sequences of color and form are visible even to the least observing. Yet at times everyone observes the moon. Such a glorious neighbor in space must have a special significance! The wonder of it has raised hundreds of questions. And now many of the answers are known.

This *How and Why Wonder Book of the Moon* takes us to the frontiers of knowledge concerning our major satellite. It summarizes much that is already known, and some of the major questions yet to be answered. Science and technology have worked hand-in-hand in spectacular ways. The great reflected-light sphere emerging in full splendor over the eastern horizon has a new meaning for everyone.

Paul E. Blackwood

Library of Congress Catalog Card No.: 76-124650

ISBN: 0-448-05068-4 (Wonder Edition)
ISBN: 0-448-04047-6 (Trade Edition)
ISBN: 0-448-03827-7 (Library Edition)
1983 PRINTING

Contents

One theory contends that the moon is a portion of the earth that was thrown-off while the earth was still semi-liquid.

According to another theory, the moon was formed from a chunk of earth torn from what is now the Pacific Ocean.

Our Neighbor in Space — the Moon

From earliest times, man has turned his eyes upward in the night to gaze at our nearest neighbor in space with wonderment and awe. The moon (for that is indeed what it is) has at various times been regarded as a mysterious object or force, a god, an omen of the weather, or of good (or bad) fortune. As seen from our own planet today, it is more often viewed merely as a beautiful sight, a celestial lamp in the night sky.

Outside of science-fiction stories, which by their very nature dwelt on fantasy and imagination, the moon was also not realistically regarded as a physically reachable goal until well past the middle of the twentieth century. The advent of the Space Age, however, changed all that, and with the assistance of rapidly changing technology man set about making plans to realize his "impossible" dream — a manned landing on the moon.

There have been a great many scientific theories about the origin of the moon. Of these, only the three most likely will be discussed here. The first holds that the moon is a thrown-off portion of the earth itself. When the earth was new

What is the origin of the moon?

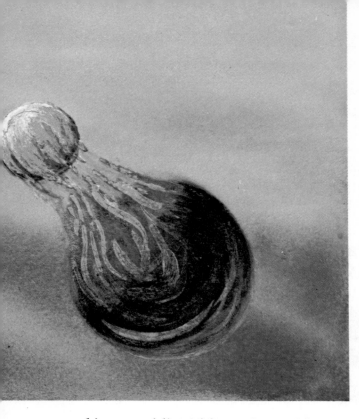

now the basin of the Pacific Ocean. About the only justification for this latter theory, most scientists think, is the fact that the total mass of the moon would just about fill the hole that is now filled by the Pacific's waters.

Other scientists believe that the moon is actually older than the earth. They contend that the moon is a relic of an earlier stage of the solar system than that during which the earth was formed. Toward the end of the earth's forma-

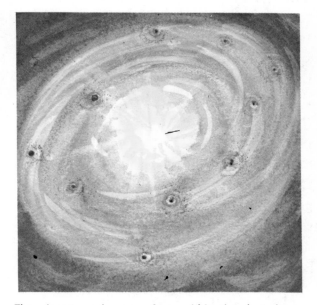

and in a semi-liquid form, its rapid revolution around the sun caused it to assume the shape of a lopsided dumbbell. The smaller part of the dumbbell broke away and became the moon.

A corollary to this theory is that after the earth had begun to solidify, a huge chunk of it was torn loose from what is

Most scientists today accept the theory that our solar system was formed from a cosmic cloud.

The planets and moons form within the dust rings.

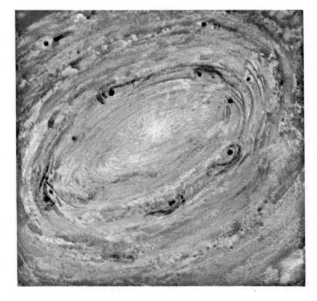

The sun forms.

Moons are captured by the planets' gravitational pull.

5

tion, it caught the moon in the force of its gravity and captured the moon as a permanent satellite.

Most scientists today, however, accept the theory that the moon and the earth were formed at the same time and of the same basic materials. They think that several billion years ago our solar system was nothing but a cloud of cold dust particles whirling aimlessly through the nothingness of deep space. Then, in response to the laws of gravity, these particles gradually came together to form a huge, spinning disk. As it spun, the disk separated into rings. The nucleus of the disk became the sun, and the particles in the outer rings became the planets. When both earth and moon had been formed, the moon, being much the smaller, was captured by the stronger gravity of the earth and so began to orbit about it just as the earth orbits around the sun. (See ill. p. 5.)

Myths about the moon

Because the moon is the nearest heavenly body to the earth, and because it appears at different times of the month in several varied forms, a great many myths and superstitions have grown up about it. Here are a few of the most common.

Many people believe that the moon affects the weather. When the moon changes, they say, the weather changes. As a result we get old-time sayings that have been handed down from generation to generation:

"Clear moon, frost soon."

"Pale moon means rain. Dark moon means winds."

"When the moon can be seen in the daytime, the days are cool."

"Frost in the dark of the moon kills buds and blossoms; frost in the light of the moon does not."

Anyone who stops to think about it soon realizes that the moon cannot possibly change the weather on earth. First, it is an inert body, a quarter million miles away, which transmits no energy except a weak reflection of the sun. In the second place, the moon can be seen over half the earth at the same time, in the tropics as well as the arctic, and obviously every place on earth does not have the same weather.

Many old-timers also believe that the moon affects the growth of seeds and plants.

"Plant beans when the moon is light."

"Plant potatoes when the moon is dark."

"Wood keeps better when cut in the new moon."

"Trees should only be pruned in the new moon."

For centuries farmers have planted and tilled their crops in accordance with these ancient rules. But no one has ever been able to prove that the moon has anything at all to do with earthly harvests.

Since long before the first history books were written, people believed that the full moon caused insanity. In fact, the word "lunacy" comes from the Latin word "luna" meaning moon. It was believed that if the full moon shone on a person while he were sleeping, that person would go mad. Another old superstition said that moonlight could cause blindness. But since moonlight is nothing more than reflected sunlight, the sun should cause a great deal more madness and blindness than the moon.

The moon has always figured prominently in both ancient and modern religion. It was worshipped as a goddess by the Greeks and Romans, as well as native tribes in Asia, Africa, Australia, and North and South America.

Today, the phases of the moon play an important part in the celebration of both Christian and Jewish Holy Days. The Christian festival of Easter always takes place on the first Sunday after the first full moon after the vernal equinox. Passover, a Jewish holiday commemorating deliverance from slavery, always falls on the first full moon of the spring, from the fourteenth to the twenty-first day of the Hebrew month Nisan.

The full moon which is nearest in date

What is the harvest moon and the hunter's moon?

to the autumnal equinox (September 23) is known as the "harvest moon." At this time, the moon rises early in the evening for three nights in succession, and is entirely or nearly full on each of the nights. Thus the light of the moon lengthens the natural period of twilight, and allows farmers extra hours of working time in which to harvest their crops before the fall frosts set in.

The "hunter's moon" follows the harvest moon, one month later, and is very similar to it. It is so called because the hunting season follows the gathering in of the crops.

There have been many fantastic tales

What was the "Great Moon Hoax"?

told about the moon. But perhaps the most ridiculous was the "great moon hoax" of 1834. The amazing thing was that most of the people of the world, including a great many leading scientists, were completely taken in by it.

It all began one afternoon when a reporter for the *New York Sun*, Richard Adams Locke, was trying to think of a sensational story to write for his paper. It had been a dull day for news. Nothing of much importance was happening in the city. So Locke let his imagination take over.

He knew that Sir John Herschel, the famous British astronomer, was making moon observations at that time from the Cape of Good Hope in Africa. That was enough of a start for the imaginative Mr. Locke. His story took it from there.

He reported that Sir John had developed a telescope twenty-four feet in diameter, which was big enough to bring the moon into view at a relative distance of 150 yards. Through it, the astronomer could see flowers, white beaches,

and a huge jewel-like rock, probably a ruby, that was 90 feet high. In a valley nearby, so went Locke's fanciful story, were herds of small bison and blue unicorns, as well as flocks of pelicans and other birds.

As the days went past, Locke's news stories grew even more fantastic. He reported the finding of two-legged beavers, horned bears, and human-like creatures that were half-man and half-bat.

After a few weeks of writing this fabulous hoax, Locke decided to quit. But by this time, the circulation of *The Sun,* which had been a small, unsuccessful paper, had ballooned into the largest in the city. Locke himself became famous, even after he had confessed that his stories were only wild figments of his imagination.

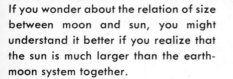

If you wonder about the relation of size between moon and sun, you might understand it better if you realize that the sun is much larger than the earth-moon system together.

The moon is "only" 6,800 miles in circumference and 2,160 miles in diameter. This means that a line drawn through its axis would extend "only" from New York to Salt Lake City.

Scientific measurement and exploration continue at various landing sites on the moon as man seeks to extend his knowledge of the events and laws of the cosmos.

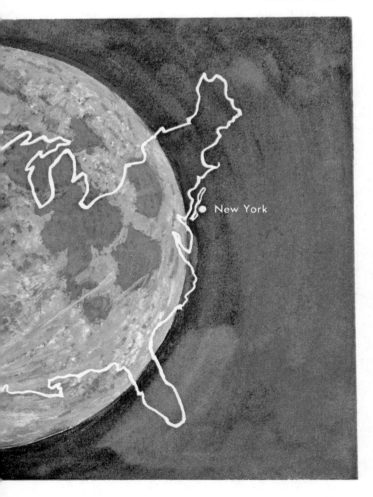

New York

The moon is 2,160 miles in diameter, roughly one-quarter the diameter of the earth. In relation to the width of the United States, this means that a line drawn through the axis of the moon would extend from New York to Salt Lake City, Utah.

How large is the moon?

The moon's mass (roughly its weight) is 1/81st that of earth's. Since the gravitational attraction of a body depends upon its mass, scientists have determined that the pull of gravity on the moon's surface is just one-sixth of that on earth. This means that if you normally weigh 150 pounds, your weight on the moon would be only 25 pounds. If you can jump three feet into the air on earth, you could jump 18 feet on the

9

moon. To use another example, if you can lift 100 pounds on earth, you could lift 600 pounds on the moon. Thus, when the first explorers reached the moon, they had minimal difficulty in lifting and transferring various scientific equipment that they had brought along with them from earth.

The moon swings around the earth in a

How far away is the moon? slightly elliptical orbit. At its *apogee*, its farthest point from earth, the moon is 252,710 miles from us. At its *perigee,* or closest point, it is 221,643 miles away. The average distance from the earth to the moon is 238,857 miles. *Apollo 11,* launched from earth, took approximately four days to reach its destination. Light from the moon reaches the earth in about one and a quarter seconds, and radio and television signals travel at the same speed. This means that a lunar explorer is able to communicate vocally almost instantly with his earth base and send back pictures.

The earth rotates on its axis once every

What are day and night on the moon? 24 hours. Thus, its average day and night are each of 12 hours duration. The moon orbits around the earth once every 27⅓ days, and in this same period it turns only once on its axis. Thus, the lunar "day" is equal to about 14 earth days, and the lunar "night" is of the same duration.

Of course, one side of the moon is *always* illuminated by the sun — just as is one side of the earth. Thus, when

it is "night" in one moon-hemisphere, it is "day" in the other.

During the "day," when the surface of the moon is fully exposed to the sun's rays, the temperature of its surface is about 220 degrees F. This is slightly higher than the boiling point of water. At "night" on the moon, the temperature plunges to about 250° F. below zero.

But since the moon has no atmosphere to absorb and transfer heat, the dark shadow cast by an overhanging rock is as cold during the "day" as it would be at "night." Thus, if you were standing on the moon with your right foot in the full sunlight, and your left foot in deep shadow, then your right foot would be exposed to 220 degree heat and your left foot to 250-below-zero cold. Fortunately, space suits worn by astronauts have 28 layers to help insulate the human body.

An astronaut on the moon, wearing his space suit.

If you could look at earth and moon from a point in space, the moon would always appear half dark. The fact that we see the various phases (inner ellipse) is caused by the changing angle under which we see the sunlit surface of the moon from our observation point on earth.

Like the earth, the moon creates no light of its own. The moonlight we see on a clear night is only a reflection of the sunlight. For this reason, the moon seems to assume different shapes at different times of the lunar month as it orbits the earth. These are called the *phases* of the moon.

Why does the moon shine?

When, in its journey around the earth, the moon comes into a direct line with the sun, we cannot see it at all. This is called the "new" moon. Twenty-four hours later, a small part of it reflects the sunlight as a thin crescent. This is commonly known as a "sickle" moon. After a week, the crescent enlarges to become a "quarter" moon. And in another week, the entire ball of the moon, or the "full" moon, is ex-posed to our view. The moon's phase then gradually recedes into the third quarter, into a crescent again, and finally into the new moon to complete once more its monthly circuit.

If you were an explorer standing on the moon and looking at the earth, you would see the same effects. The earth would shine in the reflected light of the sun, and you could properly call it "earthlight." At various phases of the earth's passage overhead, you would see "full" earth, "quarter" earth, and "crescent" earth. And, of course, at "new" earth, you could not see it at all.

The *Apollo* astronauts have already experienced the thrill of looking at their home planet and taking pictures of it. At that distance, the earth appears as a large bluish white marble.

The color of the moon, as we see it,

What color is the moon? depends upon its reflected light as it is filtered through the earth's atmosphere. Thus, in wintertime, when the moon rides higher in the sky

and its rays shine almost directly down, it appears to be white or silver. In summer, the moon moves at a lower angle across the sky and its rays are filtered through thicker layers of atmosphere. It then appears to be yellow or golden.

In his own observation of the color of the moon as seen at close range, *Apollo 11's* Edwin E. ("Buzz") Aldrin, one of earth's first moon-walkers, characterized it as "grayish cocoa" or "a very light color gray."

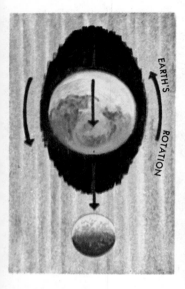

HIGH TIDE

LOW TIDE

There is a high tide and a low tide about every six hours. In other words, during approximately every 24 hours, at any point on the shore, there are two high tides and two low tides.

If you have ever been to the seashore,

How does the moon cause tides? you must have observed the daily ebb and flow of the tides. At certain time of the day, the level of the water rises sometimes as much as ten or twenty feet. A few hours later the tide has receded, leaving behind it a long stretch of empty beach. These tidal flows are caused mainly by the gravitational pull of the moon, and to a lesser degree, of the sun.

During the periods of new moon and full moon, the earth, the sun, and the

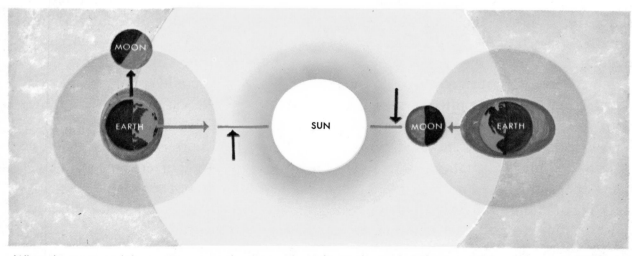

When the moon and the sun line up on the same side of the earth, or when the sun and the moon are in line, but on opposite sides of the earth, the combined gravitational pull creates unusually high or *spring tides*. When sun and moon are at right angles, the gravitational pull of each works against the other and unusually low or *neap tides* result.

12

moon are in a straight line. Thus, the moon and sun work together to cause extremely high tides, known as "spring" tides. When the moon is in its first and third quarters, it is at right angles to the sun in relation to the earth. At these times, the moon and sun are pulling against each other, resulting in lower tides, called "neap" tides.

As billions of tons of sea water are constantly being dragged back and forth across the ocean floors, the friction they create acts as a brake on the rate of the earth's rotation. And as the earth's rotation slows, the days lengthen. The result is that our days are getting about one second longer every 100,000 years.

If you attach a weight to a string and

Why does the moon stay in orbit?

swing it around your head, the weight travels in a circle. This is because two opposing

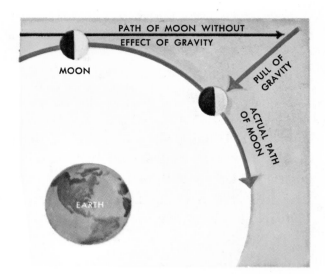

The diagram will help you to understand how and why the moon stays in orbit.

forces are working on it at the same time. A force called *tangential velocity* tends to throw the weight off in a straight line, just as the weight would do if you let go of the string. But the string, held in your hand, keeps pulling it back. Thus the weight moves in a circle.

The moon revolves in a circle around the earth in response to similar forces.

When one shore of the ocean has high tide, the other has low tide. The friction that is created by the constant dragging of billions of tons of water slows the rate of the earth's rotation.

MOON

GRAVITATIONAL PULL

LOW TIDE

HIGH TIDE

OCEAN FLOOR

The orbit of the moon becomes proportionally larger with the slowing down of the earth's rotation.

MOON

ONCE UPON A TIME
WHEN THE EARTH-DAY
WAS LESS THAN 5 HOURS.

EARTH

Hurtling along at a speed of 2,287 miles per hour, *tangential velocity* tries to fling the moon off in a straight line away from the earth. But the earth's gravity acts in the same way as the string; it keeps pulling the moon back towards the earth. Thus the moon travels serenely around us in its orbit.

It is this same principle that allows the spaceships of our astronauts to stay in an earth orbit. The outward thrust of the ship is equalized by the downward pull of the earth's gravitational force, and so the spaceship keeps going around in a circle. When the astronaut wishes to bring his vehicle back to earth, he fires a retrorocket which slows the ship's orbital speed and thus upsets this delicate relationship; then the ship falls back into the earth's atmosphere.

We have seen that the friction of the

Will the moon always stay in orbit?

tides has a braking effect upon the earth's rotation, and that as a result our days are becoming longer, at the rate of about 1/1,000th of a second a century. This rate of change is so infinitesimal that it seems absurd even to think about it. But, over future eons, it will affect the ultimate destiny of the moon, and will eventually (after countless billions of years) probably be the cause of the moon's break-up, disintegration, and death.

This tidal friction was just as effective on the earth and on the moon when both bodies were in a liquid, or semi-plastic, stage, as it is today on the waters of the earth's oceans. The result was that the moon's period of rotation on its axis became exactly the same as its period of revolution around the earth.

Now, as the earth's rotation becomes slower (even by only 1/1,000th of a second in 100 years), the orbit of the moon becomes proportionally larger. Thus the moon's distance from the earth increases, and the moon-month becomes longer.

These changes due to tidal friction have been going on for billions of years, just as they are still going on. The earth-day, which was originally less than five hours, has lengthened to 24 hours. And the moon-month, which was originally the same length as the earth-day, has increased to about four weeks.

Astronomers now calculate that the slow lengthening of the earth-day will continue until it is as long as 55 of our present days, and the moon-month will also increase to 55 of our present days. At that time, the earth will always keep the same side toward the moon, as the

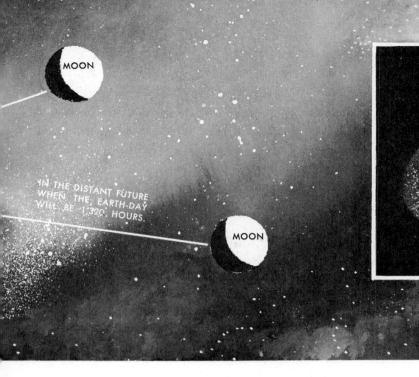

IN THE DISTANT FUTURE WHEN THE EARTH-DAY WILL BE 1,320 HOURS.

MOON

MOON

In many billions of years the moon will be pulled back toward the earth, and disintegrate upon entering the earth's atmosphere. Then its particles will form rings much like the rings around Saturn.

moon now keeps the same side toward the earth. If at that far distant time, the oceans of the earth still exist — and if they are still in a liquid state — there will be a constant high tide on the earth under the moon. Therefore there will be no more tidal friction produced by the moon. The moon and the earth will go around their common center of gravity as though locked together. The lengthening of our earth-day will cease when it has become equal to 55 of our present days.

When this balance point has been reached, the earth's rotation will gradually slow down until it is longer than the moon-month. Now the earth-moon relationship will be reversed. The earth's rotation will again speed up, and that of the moon will begin to slow down. Thus, the moon will gradually return toward the earth.

This process will continue until the moon is at last dragged down to within such a short distance of the earth that it will be broken up by the action of the earth's tidal pull. Instead of colliding with the earth, the particles of the shattered moon will collect together and form a series of rings around the earth much like the rings of the planet Saturn — although the rings will be much more massive.

But all of these amazing things will not happen until many billions of years in the future.

What is an eclipse? When the full moon moves into the deep shadow of the earth and seems to disappear, we call it the *eclipse* of the moon. There are usually one or two such lunar eclipses that are visible in the United States each year, and almost everybody has observed at least one in his lifetime. Most of us enjoy watching the spectacle of the moon being apparently swallowed up by the earth's shadow.

But in ancient times, people did not know what caused eclipses, and they were frightened by them. Even today, among some of the more primitive tribes in Africa, an eclipse causes great terror.

A story states that on his fourth voyage

How did an eclipse save Columbus?

to the New World in 1504, Christopher Columbus saved himself and his crew by his knowledge that a lunar eclipse was coming on a certain night.

Columbus badly needed supplies for his ships, but the Indians refused to get them for him. He then told the Indian chiefs that the Christian God was angry because they had refused their help; that He would punish them with famine; and that as a sign of His anger He would remove the moon from the sky.

When the eclipse began as Columbus

A lunar eclipse occurs when the moon passes through the earth's shadow. Usually in a lunar eclipse, the moon appears darkened to a deep copper red.

had said it would, the Indians were panic stricken. They promised to furnish all the provisions he wanted if he could persuade his God to give the moon back to them. When the eclipse had passed, the Indians complied.

Since astronomers are able to figure

How do lunar eclipses establish historical dates?

backwards and determine the dates of lunar eclipses in the far distant past, they have been able to establish accurate dates for many historical events.

An eclipse of the moon took place on the night before the death of the Judean King Herod who, during the final year of his reign, ordered the death of all male children in Bethlehem. He had hoped that the baby Jesus would be killed in the general slaughter. We know that this particular eclipse occurred on March 13, in the year 3 B.C. Thus we can conclude that Jesus was born at least four years before the calendar beginning of the Christian era.

The earth orbits around the sun in a

What causes an eclipse?

level plane. For example, if we suppose that the sun is in the center of a dining-room table, then the earth moves around it on the same level as the table's top. On the other hand, as the moon goes around the earth its path is tilted about five degrees. That is why we do not have an eclipse during each full moon. The earth, of course, always casts a shadow which extends nearly 859,000 miles into space, but the moon ordinarily passes above or below it. However, when the moon is in the same plane as the earth during full moon, the earth's shadow blots out the moon and an eclipse occurs.

An eclipse of the sun takes place during **What is an eclipse of the sun?** the new moon when the moon is between the earth and the sun. The shadow cast by the moon varies in length from 228,000 to 236,000 miles. For this reason, most of the times when the moon is in the right position for a solar eclipse, the moon's shadow does not reach the earth.

On the other hand, when new moon occurs during perigee (when the moon is at the lowest point in its orbit), the moon's shadow extends several thousand miles beyond the earth. On such occasions, the shadow cast by the moon onto earth may cover an area of some 475 sq. miles.

It is for the above reasons that eclipses of the sun are rare and fleeting events. They last for only a few minutes, and take place at many different points over the earth's surface. If, for example, astronomers know that a solar eclipse is scheduled to occur at Kano, in Africa, on a certain date, they will spend many many months setting up their equipment at that location in order to take photographs of the phenomenon.

In ancient China and Egypt, the high priests taught the people that when an eclipse came an evil dragon-spirit was eating up the sun, and it would disappear forever unless prayers were said and offerings were made. Other magicians and sorcerers, knowing that an eclipse was due, threatened to remove the sun from the sky unless certain of their demands were met. When the eclipse began, the people were convinced that the magician was making good his threat. After they gave him what he wanted, he would promise to make the sun reappear in a few hours, which of course it was going to do in any case.

If you are ever lucky enough to see a total solar eclipse, you will discover that it is an awe-inspiring sight. As the moon approaches the sun, the skies begin to darken as they do at normal twilight. On the farms, chickens go to roost, thinking that it is nightfall. When the moon completely obscures the sun's flaming ball, the sky becomes almost as dark as a moonless night. Then, in a

A solar eclipse occurs when the moon passes between the earth and the sun, blocking view of the sun from a section of the earth.

few minutes, the moon passes across the sun and disappears from view, and the day becomes bright again.

Ever since the dawn of history, men have been gazing up at the moon and speculating about it. Because they could see it no better than we can with the naked eye, they were not able to tell much about it. The first man who viewed a fairly good close-up image of the moon was an Italian scientist named Galileo Galilei. He is known to history by his first name.

Who was Galileo?

As a scientist, Galileo was far ahead of his time. When he was only nineteen, and a student at the University of Pisa, he observed the slow swinging of a lamp suspended from the high ceiling of a cathedral. From this he developed the theory of the pendulum, and was the first to apply it to the measure of time. According to legend, by dropping metal balls of different sizes from the leaning tower of Pisa, he proved that weight has no influence on the velocity of fall-

ing bodies. He also determined the acceleration of falling bodies.

Galileo became interested in observing the heavenly bodies, but was frustrated because he could not get a clearer look at them.

Then, in 1609, he learned that a Dutch spectacle maker named Jan Lippershey had built a gagdet that consisted of several lenses put together inside a tube. It made distant objects such as trees or people appear to be quite close. Lippershey called it the "magic tube." Galileo quickly jumped at this novel idea. He refined the lenses, adjusted their positioning inside the tube, and so built a telescope.

We can imagine how excited he was when he first turned his telescope on the moon. For the first time, he saw its craters, its mountain ranges, and its huge expanses of broad flat plains. Since these latter areas appeared smooth and featureless, as would large bodies of water, he called them seas.

For the rest of his busy life, Galileo spent a good part of his time studying the heavens. He greatly expanded his observations of the moon. He observed the dark spots on the sun through his telescope. He discovered the crescent of Venus and the four moons of Jupiter, and concluded that the hazy fog of the

Galileo, the first man to look at the moon with a magnifying telescope.

The telescope used by Galileo advanced knowledge about the moon considerably. Today, cameras mounted on powerful telescopes in our great observatories are able to take remarkably clear pictures of the surface of the moon. These cameras are capable of making accurate photographs of objects on the moon-scape that are only about a half-a-mile in length. For this reason, no major moon-mark (as compared to landmark) has gone undetected.

Milky Way actually consisted of millions of separate stars.

Of course, Galileo's first telescope was a crude and primitive affair, but it was the great grandfather of the huge telescopes that tell us so much about the moon's surface today.

Why do we see only one side of the moon?

The earth rotates on its axis in a west to east direction once every 24 hours, thus causing night and day. The moon rotates on *its* axis and in the same direction to produce night and day on the moon. But there is one great difference between the two bodies. The moon rotates on its axis only once every 27⅓ days, or, once during each time it orbits the earth.

Thus, the speed of the earth's rotation is about 1,000 miles per hour at the equator while the moon's rotation speed at its equator is only 10.35 miles per hour. These two rotation speeds are so delicately adjusted that the same half of the moon is always turned towards the earth. We call this the "earth side" of the moon. The half that we never see is called the "far side."

You can make a simple experiment that explains why we always see the same side of the moon. Place some object, such as a chair, in the center of a room, and assume for the moment that it is the earth and you are the moon. Now walk slowly around the chair in a counter-clockwise direction. When you have made one complete circle, you observe that your body has rotated once in relation to the walls of the room. But only the left side of your body has been turned toward the chair. The right side of your body has always been hidden from it.

If the moon orbited the earth in a perfect circle, we would see exactly fifty percent of its surface and no more. But since its orbit is that of a slight ellipse — that is, a little bit higher at the apogee and lower at the perigee — it appears to "wobble" in its passage.

When the moon's axis is thus tilted

toward us, we can see a few degrees beyond its north pole. When it is tilted away from us, we are able to see a few degrees beyond its south pole. In the same way, we can also observe several degrees beyond the eastern and western edges of the moon's "near side." Thus, at various times, we can see roughly sixty percent of its surface, or ten percent more than its true "earth" side.

Until 1959, no one had any definite idea

How did we first see the moon's "far side"?

at all about what the hidden side of the moon might look like. In that year, Soviet scientists successfully sent up a moon probe, called *Luna 3,* which circled the moon once. On its journey around the "far side," cameras on the craft took photographs that were transmitted back to laboratories on earth. The pictures revealed about half of the then unknown portions of the moon's surface. Though only a few formations stood out in legible detail, being too blurred to furnish accurate information, the flight was nevertheless considered significant.

On July 20, 1965, another Soviet space probe, identified as *Zond 3,* again took pictures of the moon's hidden side.

Lunar Orbiters 1 and *2,* sent up by the United States in August and November, 1966, also accomplished this mission.

Earlier United States space probes included various *Ranger* and *Surveyor* lunar spacecraft which sent back to earth thousands of close-up pictures of the moon's surface. Even before the manned landing, information on mechanically scooped-up lunar soil was made available to scientists.

The principal features of the moon's

What is the moonscape like?

surface are its mountain ranges, its craters, and its seas. Almost all of them have been given names for identification.

The sea areas, first observed by the earliest astronomers like Galileo were given Latin names: *Oceanus Procellarum* (Ocean of Storms), *Mare Imbrium* (Sea of Rains), *Mare Humorum* (Sea of Moisture), *Mare Nubium* (Sea of Clouds), *Mare Vaporum* (Sea of Vapors), *Mare Tranquillitatis* (Sea of Tranquility), *Mare Foecunditatis* (Sea of Fertility), *Lacus Somniorum* (Sea of Dreams), and many others.

For the most part, the important mountain ranges were named for mountains on earth: Alps, Apennines, Cau-

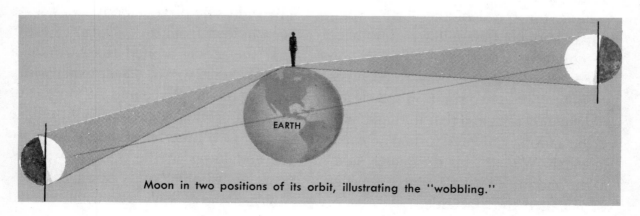

Moon in two positions of its orbit, illustrating the "wobbling."

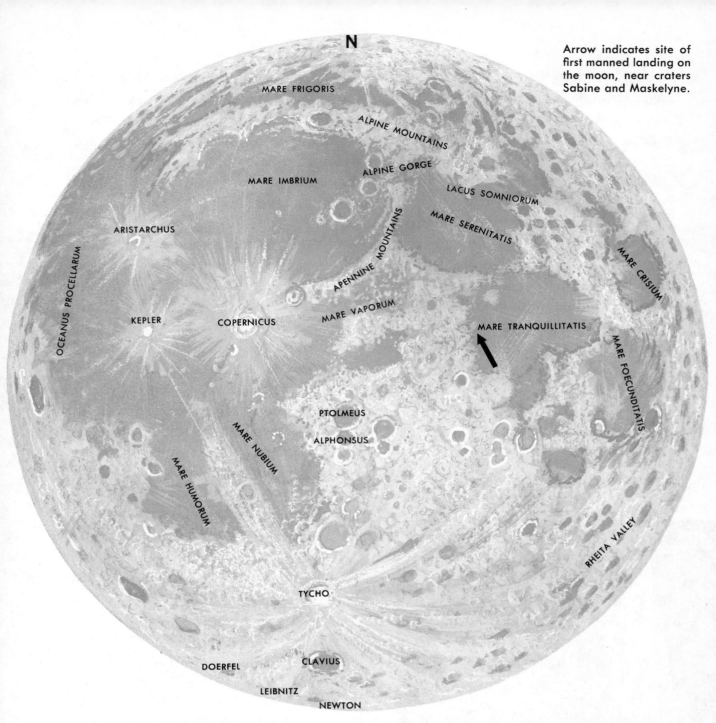

N

MARE FRIGORIS

ALPINE MOUNTAINS

ALPINE GORGE

MARE IMBRIUM

LACUS SOMNIORUM

MARE SERENITATIS

MARE CRISIUM

ARISTARCHUS

OCEANUS PROCELLARUM

APENNINE MOUNTAINS

KEPLER

COPERNICUS

MARE VAPORUM

MARE TRANQUILLITATIS

MARE FOECUNDITATIS

PTOLMEUS

ALPHONSUS

MARE NUBIUM

MARE HUMORUM

RHEITA VALLEY

TYCHO

DOERFEL

CLAVIUS

LEIBNITZ

NEWTON

The visible side of the moon. More than 30,000 craters are mapped, ranging in width from the largest, *Baily*, 183 miles in diameter, and *Clavius*, 146 miles, to the smallest photographed, ¼ mile in diameter. The deepest crater is *Newton*, 29,000 feet. The highest mountains, *Leibnitz* and *Doerfel* exceed 30,000 feet and are thus higher than the highest mountain (Everest) on earth. The largest visible valleys are *Rheita Valley*, 115 x 15 miles, and *Alpine Gorge*. The largest seas are *Mare Imbrium* (Sea of Showers) which covers about 340,000 square miles and *Oceanus Procellarum* (Ocean of Storms).

casian, Jura, Carpathian, Pyrenees. Others, such as Leibnitz and Doerfel, were named for famous astronomers.

The craters also took their names from great scientists and philosophers, both ancient and modern: Plato, Copernicus, Euclid, Archimedes, Faraday, Cavendish, Ross, Pickering, Lee, Newton, and scores of others.

When the Russians made the first charts of the moon's "far side," they named the outstanding new features which they discovered: Moscow Sea, Soviet Mountains, and Tsiolkovsky, Lomonosov, and Tsu C'hung-Chin craters.

The mountains on the moon were prob-
What are the mountains on the moon?
ably formed when the moon was in the process of changing from a liquid to a solid and its interior was molten. As it cooled, the surface wrinkled and cracked like a dried-up skin of a prune. It was in this same way that the mountains on earth were originally created.

Lacking instrumentation that can provide accurate measurements on the lunar surface, scientists can calculate the dimensions of crater ridges, mountains, etc., with the help of sharp shadows thrown on the surface by the light of the sun.

At one point, the Leibnitz Mountains tower 29,000 feet above their base. This is as high as Mt. Everest, the tallest mountain on earth. Recent calculations, which have yet to be confirmed, indicate that some moon mountains may exist which are even higher.

Altogether, some 30,000 craters have
What are the craters?
been counted on the moon. These range in size from the crater with a diameter of as much as 150 miles from rim to rim to comparatively small pock-marks fractions of a mile in diameter. The crater, Clavius, for example, is about 146 miles in diameter. To a lunar explorer standing in its center, its rims would be invisible, completely hidden from view beyond a comparatively nearby lunar horizon.

Scientists are at work theorizing exactly how these craters were created. It is believed, though, that some of the smaller ones may have been the result of volcanic activity during the moon's formative stages. Indeed, a few years ago, one astronomer observed what he believed to be an outburst of gas from the inside of the crater Alphonsus. If this observation was correct, it would indicate that the interior of the moon is still hot and gaseous, and that a possibility of volcanic activity on its surface still exists.

Since only a few lunar craters resemble earth volcanic-craters, it is supposed that most of them were caused by the tremendous impact of large meteors striking from outer space. Some scientists believe that a meteor hitting the surface of the moon at an angle would

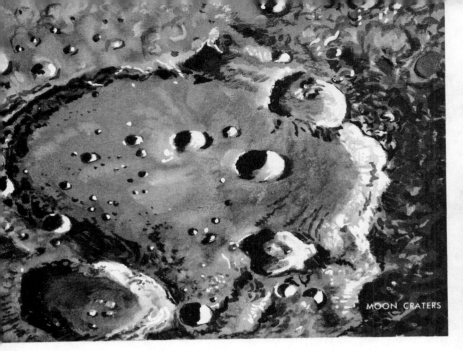

MOON CRATERS

Close-up of moon craters in the region of *Clavius* as compared with *Mount Meru Crater*, an unusually well-rounded volcanic crater on earth (Tanganyika, Africa) and meteoric craters in the United States. The comparison supports the theory that most moon craters were caused by giant meteors.

MOUNT MERU

make an elliptical crater that becomes round due to the heat of impact. Other scientists argue that whatever the angle of impact, the crater would be round. The craters on the moon are mostly round.

The size of the meteors that created the larger craters must have been enormous, triggering explosions many thousands of times greater than the most powerful nuclear bomb. The moon is constantly being bombarded by meteors, both large and small.

The earth, too, is under a constant meteor bombardment. But when a meteor approaches earth, it is burned up and vaporized as it comes into contact with the heavy layers of atmosphere. The larger ones we see as "shooting stars." Sometimes, if the meteor is originally large enough, a small core of it survives and lands on earth as a chunk of metal.

But since the moon has no atmosphere, a meteor can strike it with full force, and thus gouge out a big depression on the surface.

METEORIC CRATERS IN AMERICA

The winds and waters of earth are constantly at work to change the earth's surface and erase the marks of its geologic history. But the moon is without the erosive effects of wind and water. Thus, it is almost certain that every scar inflicted on the lunar surface remains exactly as it was when it was first made.

Some of the circle-craters, like *Copernicus* for instance, have huge central peaks and show conspicuous landsliding of the inner slope.

Scientists have not observed any new craters of appreciable size that have been created on the moon since the invention of the telescope. From this we might conclude that the meteoric bombardment of the moon — especially by giant meteors — has not been as great in the last few hundred or few thousand years as it was in the distant past.

Rilles are less prominent features of

What are rilles?

the lunar surface — long narrow trenches, some shallow, some deep, located near the circular seas. Characteristically they form a wandering path extending from one or two miles to several hundred. They may have been formed by flowing lava.

One of the most puzzling mysteries of

What are the "rays"?

the moonscape are the rays. These are bright streaks that fan out in all directions from some of the bigger craters, notably Tycho, Copernicus and Kepler, and from many of the smaller ones as well. Some of these rays emanating from Tycho are so long that they extend more than a thousand miles.

No one has ever been able to determine just how these rays were originally formed, or what they consist of. The most popular theory is that they are long streamers of rock fragments that were scattered by the meteors that formed the craters.

You can see how this might have happened if you place a small pile of fine face powder on a piece of dark paper and then strike it sharply with the round side of a spoon. The powder will fly out in all directions in precisely the same pattern as that of the rays we can see on the moon.

Since there is no air or wind on the moon to disturb these dust patterns, they would have remained exactly as they were when they were originally made.

Another theory holds that the rays may be composed of a lighter-colored sublunar material that was blasted from the crater by the meteor. The heat of the meteor's impact and explosion may have melted and fused this material into a glass-like form. Such glass particles would reflect light, and thus might account for the fact that rays vary in brightness as phases of moon change.

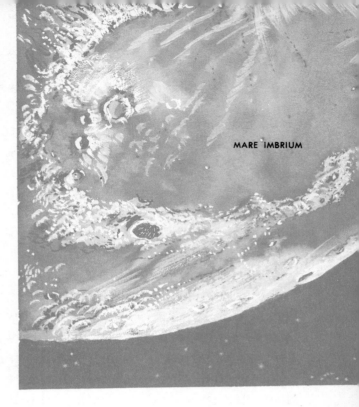

The seas, like the *Mare Imbrium* shown here, have no water. At top left, are the *Apennine Mountains*.

MARE IMBRIUM

The great level plain areas of the moon are called "seas." The
What are the "seas"? earliest astronomers, gazing at the moon with their primitive telescopes, did not know that the moon was a lifeless, waterless body, and reasoned that parts of its surface must be covered by water like the seas on earth. We know now that the "seas" are dust-covered deserts, but they have been allowed to keep their original designations as "seas." And indeed at one time, when the moon was being formed, they were probably actual seas of molten lava.

Since the "seas" are flat and apparently less hostile than the more rugged mountain areas of the moonscape, the Sea of Tranquility became the site of the first manned landing by *Apollo 11's* lunar module *Eagle*.

The rays emanating from the bigger craters are puzzling mysteries. Shown here is *Tycho* with rays extending more than 2,000 miles from the crater and disappearing over the horizon into the moon's far side.

Does the moon contain valuable minerals?

The metal products of the earth are gradually diminishing, and though it may be thousands of years before such resources are completely exhausted, government and industry are already looking to the deposits on the moon to provide raw materials for earth's uses well into the distant future.

Thus far, examination of the lunar rocks and soil brought to earth by *Apollo* astronauts, combined with earlier data obtained from instruments on *Surveyor* and other spacecraft, discloses that elements approximating those found in basalt rock on earth are present. Most of the lunar rocks analyzed have been basalts, yet they differ from those found on earth in that they have a higher titanium and iron content, and less water, oxygen and other volatile substances. Other chemical elements known to be on the moon in varying quantities are silicon, sulfur, aluminum, magnesium, scandium and vanadium.

Photo of moon's surface taken by Surveyor I, June, 1966. It shows a rock, approximately 6 inches high by 18 inches long, lying a few feet from Surveyor I on the lunar surface.

Do air and water exist on the moon?

If we accept the most popular scientific theory, namely that the moon and earth were formed at the same time and of the same basic material, then we can theorize that they probably followed the same basic pattern of evolution. In this case, the moon once had an atmosphere, and also a form of water.

Why, then, if this atmosphere and water remained on the earth, did it not also remain on the moon? Most scientists believe that the answer lies in the difference between the force of the earth's gravity and that of the moon's.

The pull of the earth's gravity keeps our atmosphere and water from escaping into space as the earth rotates. But the moon's gravitational pull was not strong enough to hold onto its own atmosphere. Therefore, over millions of years, its air and moisture escaped into the void of space.

There is, however, a trace of atmosphere on the moon: a few gaseous molecules that cling to cracks in the surface. At the most generous estimate, this atmosphere amounts to no more than one-millionth that of the atmosphere on the earth's surface. This would roughly be equal to the air pressure that exists seventy miles above the earth. For all practical purposes, the moon has been shown to be an extremely hot and cold, airless, waterless globe.

Our modern explorers, of course, were provided with space suits that shielded them from the extremes of heat and cold, the total lack of air pressure, and other basic dangers. A portable life support system provided oxygen.

Since the moon is airless and waterless,

Does life exist on the moon? it was generally concluded that it is also entirely lifeless. However, as in most things concerning the moon, there were differences of opinion.

Some scientists proposed that the changes in color that occurred in certain moon craters might be due to a species of vegetation that grew there during the hot moon-day. Presumably, if such vegetation existed, it froze during the cold moon-night, and then came back to life when the sun shined again. This cycle would be comparable to that of trees on earth, which appear lifeless during the winter, and leaf and blossom again in the spring.

One astronomer observed moving patches on at least one of the crater floors. He reasoned that these might be swarms of some kind of insects, feeding on the vegetation.

The first exploration team sent to the moon was given scientific assignments ranging from simple to ambitious to test for any form of sheltered life that might actually exist below the surface.

For many centuries man had dreamed

Why did we want to explore the moon? a wistful dream of someday going to the moon. But it was not until the development of such tremendously powerful launch vehicles as the *Saturn V* rocket and the *Apollo* spacecraft that such an attempt became feasible. Years of careful planning by both the United States National Aeronautics and Space Administration (NASA) and the Soviet space agency, extensive training of the men who were to be sent on moon missions, and costs representing an investment of billions of dollars were all expended and directed toward the achievement of that elusive goal.

Quarantine chest containing samples of lunar rock and soil brought to earth by the crew of the *Apollo 11* is unloaded from plane by elated NASA officials prior to transfer of the specimens to the Lunar Receiving Laboratory.

Many people have questioned whether the expenditure of billions of dollars to land teams of explorers on the moon was justified.

It is true that astronomers were able to learn much about the moon by using telescopes and radar beams, but there was much more that these devices could not disclose. Scientists wanted to find out what kind of rocks, ores, minerals and elements the moon contained; what the soil of the moon was like; whether there was any kind of dormant life present; what the exact effect of solar radiation was upon the lunar surface; whether the moon contained subsurface moisture.

The answers to these and other questions were sought to provide further answers as to the origin and evolution of our ancient satellite, the moon, and thus perhaps furnish clues relating to the birth of our own planet, our own solar system — yes, even our own galaxy!

The instruments of unmanned spacecraft can measure conditions and characteristics both on the moon and in space by which scientists can deduce certain facts, but they are limited in that they can only do what they have been built to do. They cannot cope with the unexpected. Only man's judgment can attempt to handle the unforeseen.

Early attempts at exploring the moon by unmanned space probes were, for the most part, failures. Moonbound spacecraft either fell back to earth, missed the moon, or crashed violently upon the moon's surface, demolishing all instrumentation on board. The first notably successful lunar probe of this kind took place on October 4, 1959 (two years to the day after the launching of the Soviet *sputnik,* which inaugurated the Space Age), when the Soviet Union sent forth a spacecraft known as *Luna 3,* which circled the moon and sent back to earth pictures of the moon's far side. It was the first time that man had ever had a chance to study or even observe the hidden side of the moon.

Failure dogged the moon-probe programs for the following six years, but then the United States achieved three brilliant successes as *Rangers 7, 8* and *9* took superbly clear pictures of the moon's surface at fairly close range.

On January 31, 1966, the Soviets sent *Luna 9* to the moon. Rockets fired as the craft approached its destination slowed its speed so that its landing was not as destructive as those of its predecessors. *Luna 9* carried a shockproof camera which sent back to earth nine pictures taken on the moon's surface.

In June, 1966, a United States spacecraft, *Surveyor 1,* made a really soft landing on the moon and transmitted thousands of pictures which indicated that the moon's surface was not generally a thick layer of dust.

During the next few months the Soviet Union launched four spacecraft to orbit the moon and send back pictures and scientific data. Three of these craft carried out successful missions. The United States sent three moon-orbiting

Artist's conception of a moon-city. Fantastic? Yes. But less so than Jules Verne's novel in 1874 "*From the Earth to the Moon.*" One of the illustrations of the novel showed the moonship after landing, and the passengers observing the universe (see inset).

camera craft on survey missions — and they all transmitted detailed pictures.

With the advent of manned landings and human exploration, scientists have been able to accelerate their studies of the lunar surface by first-hand analysis and examinations of samplings of rocks and soil brought back to earth by our conscientious astronauts. The *Apollo 11* explorers, Armstrong and Aldrin, collected about sixty pounds of lunar soil and rocks during their two-hour stay on the moon, sealed the specimens in chests aboard the LM *Eagle* to preserve their natural characteristics, and literally hand-delivered them upon their return. Many of the rocks brought back from the moon were coated with a fine, graphite-like cocoa-colored powder. Microscopic examination indicated a mixture of olivine, pyroxine and feldspar, a basic resemblance to volcanic rocks.

It has always been the nature of man to explore the unknown. Because of this urge, early seafarers found the New World; American pioneers discovered and developed the great country that lay over the western mountains; Arctic adventurers opened both the north and south polar areas to exploration.

A famous mountain climber was once asked why he wanted to scale the dangerous heights of Mount Everest. He replied simply: "Because it is there." That was undoubtedly one of the reasons why men wanted to land on the moon. Just because it is there.

Does the moon have any new minerals?

Mineralogists who have assisted in examining the lunar rocks brought to earth have discovered at least three new minerals unknown on earth. The names by

Rockets developed by the United States in the Space Age include (left to right): (1) the *Atlas*, used to send astronauts into orbit around the earth in *Project Mercury*; the *Titan*, used to perfect "docking" (joining-up) techniques in *Project Gemini*; the *Saturn C-1*, used to test *Apollo* components; and the *Saturn V*, used for *Project Apollo*, the manned landing on the moon. These launch vehicles are compared in size with the Washington Monument in Washington, D. C., towering 555 feet. The *Saturn V* is higher (by fifty feet or more) than the Statue of Liberty in New York Harbor.

Stations throughout the world such as the one shown in the illustration above, help track space vehicles and send flight information to a central computer. At left, an *Apollo* space vehicle is shown mounted on launch complex 39-A.

which these minerals will be known are pyroxmangite, chromium-titanium spinel and ferropseudobrookite.

The Sea of Tranquility, where the first men from earth landed to collect samples of lunar soil, appears to be particularly high in titanium. This is borne out not only by analysis of the samples at the landing site, but by previous analysis of data obtained from *Surveyor 5,* situated about twenty miles away. The comparatively rich content of this metal on the moon — seemingly higher than that found in earth rocks or meteorites — may prove to be both significant and valuable for scientific and commercial purposes.

What was the "black box" group?

When discussions first took place by scientists as to the best or most practical means of obtaining information through space probes, opinions seemed to differ. There were some who contended that man himself would have to observe what could be

seen, experience what could be felt, and transmit back to earth what could be learned. Those who believed this course to be best became known as the "warm body" group. In short, they favored the man-in-space program which was later to give birth to Projects *Mercury, Gemini* and *Apollo.*

But there were also those who believed that non-manned or mechanical exploration should be emphasized, at least in the beginning. These people were known as the "black box" group. They inclined toward the projects which

31

came to be called *Ranger, Surveyor, Lunar Orbiter* and *Lunar Explorer*.

When Christopher Columbus set sail

What were the first moon probes?

across the watery expanse of the Atlantic Ocean, he and his men had to "play it by ear" — that is to say, they had to find out all the answers for themselves through the use of their own five senses. It was somewhat different for the men who were to be our moon pioneers. In order to eliminate as much of the guesswork and danger as possible before the first men tried for a landing, the National Aeronautics and Space Administration (NASA), the space agency of the United States, planned its own careful program of first sending out numerous *unmanned* spacecraft — vehicles crammed with scientific instruments which would relay vital information (notably pictures) back to earth.

Two early vehicles sent out by the United States failed. The first one missed the moon by about 22,000 miles and went into permanent orbit around the sun. The second one lost its power.

The first unmanned moon probes planned by NASA were known as *Rangers*. There were several types on the drawing boards. One of them was designed to eject a blue-and-white ball, about half again as large as a basketball, made of segments of balsa, the lightest and most resilient of all woods, while the main vehicle was some 70,000 feet above the moon. The ball itself would contain a seismometer, an earthquake (or, in this case, a moonquake) recorder, and a radio transmitter.

Dropping to the moon after being temporarily slowed or stopped by the retro-rocket ejection at a moon-altitude of approximately one thousand feet, the ball was expected to record the number and size of meteorites striking the moon; reveal whether the lunar surface was firm and hard enough to sustain a large-craft landing (as for one holding astronauts); and determine whether or not the moon was inert.

The United States was not the only

What were the Soviet lunar spacecraft?

country dedicated to a program of exploring space and the planets in general, and of sending men and instruments to the moon in particular. Russia (the Union of Soviet Socialist Republics) was also involved. For reasons stemming chiefly from opposing political ideologies and a reluctance to exchange technological information that might usurp a real or supposed military advantage, the two countries preferred to work in competition, rather than in concert. Unrealized were the obvious advantages of lessened costs and greater progress to be derived from mutual cooperation and assistance — it was not to be.

The Soviet Union must certainly be credited with some notable "firsts" of their own in space probes, ventures and techniques. On the last day of January, 1966, for example, at a launching site east of the Aral Sea, the Russians sent into space a vehicle that would have the distinction of making the first controlled "soft" landing on the moon. Such landings, which lower craft comparatively gently to the lunar surface by means of retrorockets, needed to be established and demonstrated as feasible before man himself could make the attempt.

This particular mooncraft was known as *Lunar 9*, and as it blasted off on its historic trip from the launching pad at Cosmodrome Zvesdograd (a counterpart to the United States' John F. Kennedy Space Center), the fiery tail of the rocket turned the surrounding snow into steam. Watching the liftoff, technicians and cosmonauts (the name the Russians give to the men whom we call astronauts) wondered whether this mission would be any different from at least four earlier attempts to land instruments the "soft" way, which had failed.

With two-thirds of *Lunar 9's* first orbit around the earth completed, the velocity of the craft was boosted to permit it to escape the gravitational pull of the earth. Then the 3,500-pound vehicle, containing a 220-pound automatic sta-

Destination moon!

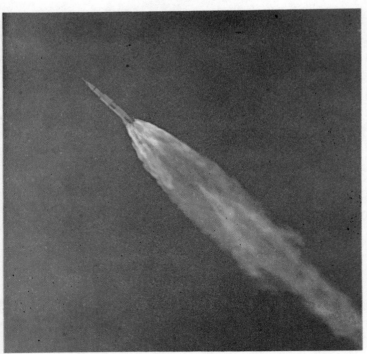

tion for transmitting scientific data, was on its way, its destination the Ocean of Storms, near the lunar equator. A correction of trajectory was made in midcourse by radio, and *Luna 9* obeyed, aligning itself by means of an optical system that sought out both the light of the sun and the reflected light of the moon.

Firing the retrorockets with which the vehicle was equipped for precisely the right interval (48 seconds), at precisely the right distance from the moon (a lunar altitude of 46.6 miles) altered velocity to near-zero. Just before final contact, the instrument package separated to fall on its own shock-absorbent material, its impact reduced still more by the moon's weak gravitational pull. Then, like unfolding petals of a flower, four sections of the outer housing opened up, exposing a television camera in a predetermined upright position, and soon the first long-awaited close-up pictures of the moon's surface were on their way to earth. They disclosed a porous surface and some small rocks. There was no perceptible thick layer of moondust.

Two months after this noteworthy event, the Soviets

How did Luna 10 prove the value of space probes?

launched *Luna 10,* which turned out to be a lunar-orbiting spacecraft, traveling an elliptical course that ranged from 217 miles to 621 miles from the surface. It was another astounding space "first." Imagine — the first modern man-made satellite revolving around the earth's own ancient and natural satellite, the moon!

Luna 10 carried instruments to measure the moon's gravity, its radiation, and its magnetic fields. It also collected data on meteorite activity, recording a concentration of micrometeorite hits that was about a hundred times greater in the vicinity of the moon at that time than had occurred earlier in the course of getting there. More significantly, *Luna 10* detected a basaltic lunar surface by means of gamma-ray emanations, which led numerous scientists to the conclusion that the moon was once molten, and that its origin was the same as the earth's.

With each elliptical orbit, *Luna 10* was able to obtain more scientific information about the moon than had been gained in years of study and observation before space probes became a reality.

The Sea of Tranquility area, landing site for the first men on the moon.

What were the Surveyors? Spurred on by the accomplishments of the Soviet's instrumented exploration of the moon, yet forced to develop methods and operational techniques of its own, the United States eventually got its long-delayed machine-on-the-moon program "off the ground," too. It was called *Surveyor*.

Surveyor 1 was a 594-pound spacecraft (it would weigh but 99 pounds on the moon) set atop an *Atlas-Centaur* rocket that burned for a little over seven minutes as it headed directly for the moon. Its solar panels and antennas were extended a scant twenty minutes into the flight, and its course was accurately aligned from sightings of the sun and the bright star Canopus.

The coasting speed of *Surveyor 1* accelerated from three thousand miles per hour to six thousand miles per hour as it approached the moon. But about sixty miles from its eventual destination, the spacecraft began its landing preparations: it extended its large "music-stand"-type legs (which terminated in crushable aluminum foot pads) toward the target and the braking rocket fired, causing the gases from the retrorocket to assume, in the vacuum of space, a balloonlike shape. Smaller engines that began operating decelerated the craft's speed even more, so that when the first *Surveyor* finally made its perfect landing in an eroded crater on the western side of the moon, it was ready and able to carry out a scientific job, its impact having been comparatively negligible. The date was June 2, 1966. Across the Ocean of Storms was the site of the first soft landing on the moon — but the Soviet Union's *Luna 9* was only a silent signpost now, its instruments having been alternately baked and frozen beyond use by the moon's merciless temperature extremes.

Though *Surveyor 1* lacked some of the basic instrumentation of the earlier *Luna 9*, it was equipped with (1) efficient solar panels that recharged batteries for nearly two weeks after the landing and (2) a superbly functioning television camera that recorded photographic details of the lunar surface with excellent quality. During its workable lifetime (before the intolerable sub-zero temperatures of the lunar night could take effect), more than eleven thousand pictures were taken and sent back to earth. They included scenes of a distant lunar mountain range and close-ups of the granular grayish "moon sand" which, it was conjectured, could have been caused by the smashing of exposed rocks by meteorites.

What did later Surveyors do? More *Surveyors* followed *Surveyor 1* to the moon. Not all were successful—*Surveyor 2* and *Surveyor 4* crashed. But others accomplished what they were sent there for — the gathering of scientific data.

Surveyor 3 landed on the moon on April 19, 1967. Perhaps it would be more accurate to say that it "bounced," since the retrorockets were still firing at the first touchdown and had the effect of lifting the craft off the surface. When this action was stopped by radio command from earth, however, *Surveyor 3* settled down to business within the relatively small crater it now found itself.

There a mechanical arm dug small trenches in the lunar soil, which by all indications had the measured "feeling" of damp sand. A number of bearing and impact tests were conducted, as well.

On September 10, 1967, *Surveyor 5* made its landing on the moon by way of a skid down a crater, almost but fortunately not quite toppling over in the process, and two months later *Surveyor 6* hit a rougher, ridged surface than any previously detected. What made these two *Surveyors* significant was that alpha particles, scattered near the landing site, were used as a means of determining what chemical elements were present on the moon. Chemical analysis of the surface material at both landing sites showed a basaltic rock composition.

Unlike the previous *Surveyors* which were sent to the equatorial region of the moon, *Surveyor 7* was directed to the highlands near a crater in the moon's southern hemisphere known as Tycho. It narrowly missed a large rock as it landed. By this time, the *Surveyor* craft had become quite versatile. This one held magnets for picking up iron, a mechanical digging arm, a device for scattering alpha particles, a television camera, and other features. An unscheduled "remote-control repair job" to free the chemical analyzer for proper emplacement became a spectacular achievement in its own right.

The chemical composition of the highlands on the moon, it was found, was different from the *maria,* the smoother, more level lowlands. To some geologists on earth, this difference was significant, suggesting that the moon was once in a molten state.

What were the Lunar Orbiters? America's exploratory space ventures continued with the "third-generation class" of unmanned spacecraft designed specifically for gaining information about the moon, the *Lunar Orbiters.* The *Rangers* were sent to the moon on a kind of *kamikaze* or suicide mission — that is, to crash-land on target, but to take as many pictures of the moon as possible along the way. This they did, successively producing photographs of greater quality and detail. Soft-landing *Surveyors* "went them one better" by sending close-up pictures directly from the lunar surface, but again, the area to be observed and studied was fairly limited. It was necessary to obtain a more overall picture of the lunar surface, particularly along the moon's equator, which seemed to offer the smoothest possible sites, before manned landings could be attempted. *Lunar Orbiters* would — and did — provide this picture, as well as much related useful information, beginning in August, 1966.

How did the U.S. "man-in-space" program develop? As the "black box" group continued to gain much new information about the moon from their non-manned or mechanical exploration vehicles, the "warm body" group was not idle. "A man, with his brains," one astronaut declared, "is the cheapest computer that NASA can send to the moon." Of course, he was not talking about just any man. He was referring to a man such as himself, someone highly trained and motivated, a combination physicist, astronomer, geologist and spacecraft mechanic.

To send men to the moon, the United States arranged for three distinct projects—*Project Mercury, Project Gemini,* and *Project Apollo.* Each project had its own series of flights — and each flight was calculated to be more difficult, more ambitious, and more daring than its predecessor. In general, the first of these projects, *Project Mercury,* would carry a single astronaut into suborbital flight; the second project, *Project Gemini,* would call for two men in a capsule, marathon (endurance) orbits,

"space walks," joining or "docking" with other space vehicles, and various tests of equipment and maneuvering techniques; and *Project Apollo,* carrying three men, would culminate in manned exploration of the moon.

Following a series of successful flights in *Apollo* space-craft that proved the efficacy of disciplined, well-trained men and of rigidly tested equipment, NASA officials at last judged that the time was ripe for a manned orbit of the moon. A sobering and sorrowful incident — the unexpected deaths of three gallant astronauts, Virgil "Gus" Grissom, Edward H. White II, and Roger Chaffee, in a flash fire within an *Apollo* command module on the ground — had had a demoralizing and delaying effect on the program, but it had also precipitated a reappraisal of the safety standards, bringing about the installation of new fire-resistant materials.

What was man's first flight to the moon?

Accordingly, early in the morning on December 21, 1968, a tremendous 278-foot *Saturn 5* rocket lifted off Pad 39A at Cape Kennedy in a shattering burst of sound and flame. At the front end of the elongated inferno, within a thirteen-foot *Apollo* command module, were three mortal men: Frank Borman, William Anders, and James Lovell.

Somewhere over Australia on its second revolution, *Apollo 8* was given the order from Mission Control in Houston, Texas, to "go for the moon" — and go it did, as the third-stage rocket burned for over five minutes with 225,000 pounds of thrust. The historic

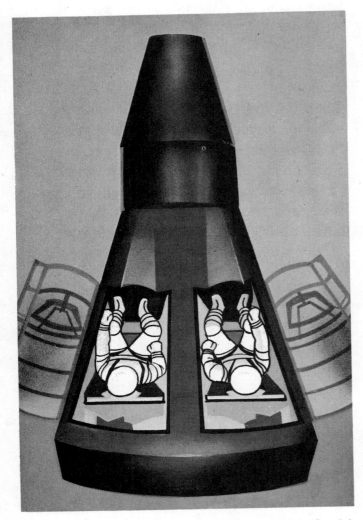

Cutaway view of training capsule of *Project Gemini.*

journey was under way, the spacecraft traveling at the incredible speed of 24,600 miles an hour. It was the greatest rate of speed ever experienced by any man. Sixty-six hours or so later the astronauts were farther away from their home planet than any man had gone before. Yet they were less than seventy miles above the moon's surface!

All of the fantastic dreams were coming true, and everything was taking place, still incredibly so, as predicted.

None the less remarkable were views of the solar corona, lunar sunrises and sunsets, and — possibly most impressive of all — the home planet of earth, a bluish-white marble in three-quarters phase, peeking over the lunar horizon.

Only a few short years before manned moon shots became **How are manned** a reality, space ex-**moon landings** perts were in dis-**made possible?** agreement as to the most feasible method of putting a man on the moon. Wernher von Braun and several other notable rocket scientists were inclined to accomplish this by first having two giant Saturn rockets orbit the earth. One of these would carry the astronauts, the other, extra fuel. When the two units joined in flight, the astronauts would simply take on the extra fuel and then launch themselves on the lunar path.

A NASA engineer, John C. Houbolt, believed that such plans were both too expensive and too involved. He visualized an audacious, yet direct and simplified, approach which has now become known as Lunar Orbit Rendezvous (LOR). His concept—ridiculed at first by his associates who may have been steeped in sophisticated technology — was to place an *Apollo* spacecraft directly into lunar orbit and then detach a smaller lunar module capable of lowering itself safely to the surface and also launching itself to a return rendezvous with the orbiting mother ship.

The practicality of this scheme was eventually conceded by NASA officials, and thus the lunar module (LM) was born, a space vehicle appearing so cumbersome that it seemed to have been thrown together with a collection of spare parts. But utility was the primary concern, not beauty — and utility is what resulted. Twenty-five layers of wrinkled aluminized sheets cover the craft. On half the surface, in addition, there is a thicker, firm top sheet. On the other half is a wrinkled flimsy sheet. These varied thicknesses of insulation ward off extremes of hot and cold. The module's shape is closer to a bug's than a machine's, but form was not the object in its creation. The LM was designed to accommodate and protect the most sensitive and vital of equipment — and, at all costs, man.

With Colonel Thomas P. Stafford, Commander John W. **What was** Young, and Com-**Apollo 10's** mander Eugene A. **mission?** Cernan aboard, *Apollo 10* blasted off from Cape Kennedy on May 18, 1969, in a final rehearsal for the lunar landing. Combining the features of its two immediate predecessors, *Apollo 10* managed to go a little further in all departments. This time the lunar module came to within 9.4 miles of the

An *Apollo* space vehicle carrying men to the moon starts its journey with an overture of fire and fury as it lifts off the earth.

moon's surface and circled the moon's equator thirty-one times in two and a half days, compared with the ten orbits of *Apollo 8.* This time the lunar module and the command ship engineered a link-up about sixty-nine miles from the moon, 230,000 miles from earth. And this time there were color television pictures, photographs of the intended lunar landing site on the Sea of Tranquility, and extensive tests of the effect of the moon's weak gravitational pull.

Said Dr. Thomas O. Paine, NASA administrator, soon after the three elated astronauts stepped onto the red-carpeted deck of the carrier U.S.S. *Princeton,* "We know we can go to the moon. We will go to the moon."

And go they did. On July 17, 1969, at 9:32 A.M., before a million persons jammed into the Cape Kennedy area and many other millions throughout the world glued to television sets that focused on the 363-foot vehicle on launching pad 39-A, *Apollo 11,* in a burst of smoke and flame, roared and lifted off. Neil Armstrong, Lieutenant Colonel Michael Collins, and Colonel Edwin E. ("Buzz") Aldrin — together with the command

How did *Apollo 11* start out?

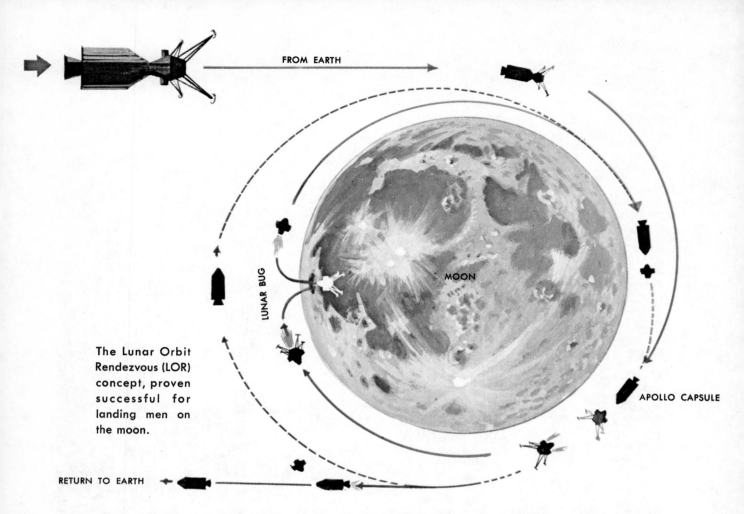

FROM EARTH

LUNAR BUG

MOON

APOLLO CAPSULE

RETURN TO EARTH

The Lunar Orbit Rendezvous (LOR) concept, proven successful for landing men on the moon.

ship *Columbia* and the lunar module *Eagle* — were destined to become part of man's historic first walk on the moon. Tension mounted with each rocket-firing and operational phase as *Apollo 11* sped toward its space target.

As the spacecraft swirled into its eleventh orbit of the moon, astronauts Armstrong and Aldrin, wearing their white, bulky pressurized suits, left Michael Collins alone in the command module and crawled through a connecting tunnel to the lunar module. Then came the undocking. *Eagle* was released from *Columbia* and began its descent.

What was the "giant leap for mankind"?

At 4:17 P.M. (E.D.T.), July 20, 1969, these words, the first from the moon, were spoken by Armstrong: "Houston, Transquility Base here. The *Eagle* has landed." Six and a half hours later, about four hours ahead of schedule, Neil Armstrong gingerly placed his left foot on the brownish lunar surface and announced, "That's one small step for a man, one giant leap for mankind." Nineteen minutes later Armstrong was joined by Aldrin, the second man to set foot on the moon.

In virtually effortless fashion, loping like playful baby kangaroos amid what Aldrin had termed "a magnificent desolation," the two men scooped up about sixty pounds of soil and rock samples for analysis. They set up a miniature seismic station for transmitting data on possible tremors or

What were man's first placements on the moon?

moonquakes. They erected a reflector to bounce laser beams back to earth. They put up — and later took down — a banner of aluminum foil facing the sun that would detect the nuclei of such gases as neon, argon and krypton.

Plans and preparations for *Apollo 12* were already under way, even as the *Apollo 11* astronauts, their fame now assured in the annals of space travel, headed for a safe splashdown in the Pacific Ocean. The astronauts who would take part in the *Apollo 12* mission were Commander

What was Apollo 12's mission?

Charles Conrad, Jr., and Alan L. Bean, these two assigned to walk the lunar surface, and Commander Richard F. Gordan, slated to remain in the orbiting command module.

In the LM *Intrepid* astronauts Conrad and Bean separated from the command module *Yankee Clipper*. It was 1:54 A.M. (E.D.T.), November 19, 1969, when this second party of lunar explorers set down their craft almost exactly on the spot aimed for in the Ocean of Storms. The *Intrepid* was 950 miles west of *Apollo 11's* Tranquility Base and within close walking distance of *Surveyor 3*, the unmanned U.S. spacecraft

Components of the lunar module.

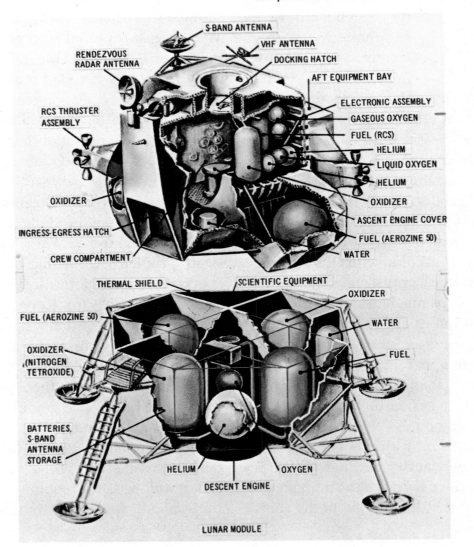

S-BAND ANTENNA
VHF ANTENNA
RENDEZVOUS RADAR ANTENNA
DOCKING HATCH
AFT EQUIPMENT BAY
ELECTRONIC ASSEMBLY
RCS THRUSTER ASSEMBLY
GASEOUS OXYGEN
FUEL (RCS)
HELIUM
LIQUID OXYGEN
HELIUM
OXIDIZER
OXIDIZER
ASCENT ENGINE COVER
INGRESS-EGRESS HATCH
FUEL (AEROZINE 50)
CREW COMPARTMENT
WATER
THERMAL SHIELD
SCIENTIFIC EQUIPMENT
OXIDIZER
FUEL (AEROZINE 50)
WATER
OXIDIZER (NITROGEN TETROXIDE)
FUEL
BATTERIES, S-BAND ANTENNA STORAGE
HELIUM
OXYGEN
DESCENT ENGINE

LUNAR MODULE

that had been on the moon since September, 1967. The astronauts brought back parts of *Surveyor 3* in order to determine first-hand the effects of the lunar environment.

Besides picking up parts of *Surveyor 3,* astronauts Conrad and Bean collected nearly a hundred pounds of rock samples and soil, and experimentally tossed some rocks in order to obtain seismological readings. Among the equipment they left on the moon was a scientific observatory with a nuclear power plant that was expected to transmit data over an extended period of time.

When the *Apollo 12* moon samples were

What was Apollo 12's "prize" rock? brought to the Manned Spacecraft Center, they did not appear to be significantly different. Only when they were processed by the radiation counting laboratory was it disclosed that one particular lemon-sized moon rock seemed to possess an unusually high degree of natural (harmless) radiation. Scientists set it aside for a closer look. Subsequent analysis revealed that the rock, which was light gray in color, with cloudy white crystals and dark gray streaks, contained twenty times as much uranium, thorium and potassium as any other lunar rock. The conclusion reached was that the rock had an apparent age of 4.6 billion years, older than any rock found on earth, and suggested that it might date from "the year one"—the actual birth of our solar system, with all of its planets. Just as significantly, the find indicates that the surface layers of the moon have changed very little throughout the eons.

The flight of *Apollo 13,* carrying Navy

How did the first crippled spaceship return? Captain James A. Lovell, Jr. (who had earlier participated in the moon-orbiting *Apollo 8*), and civilian space rookies Fred W. Haise, Jr. and John L. Swigert, Jr., was not able to fulfill its $350 million mission, that of gathering additional samples of lunar rock in the Fra Mauro area. Unexpecedly, 205,000 miles from the earth on its path to the moon, the spacecraft was rocked by an explosion. The main power supply in the service module *Odyssey* was damaged and the life-sustaining oxygen within the command module was rapidly spilling out into the void, due to ruptured storage tanks.

The crisis made it apparent immediately that the scheduled moon landing would have to be abandoned. All efforts would have to be directed exclusively toward the safe return of the astronauts to earth. At Mission Control, in Houston, Texas—and elsewhere—hundreds of experts in aerospace technology, assisted by millions of dollars worth of computers, grappled with the life-or-death problem of utilizing the disabled spacecraft's capabilities to the fullest.

As a first measure, to neutralize the bucking, spinning, tumbling action of the spacecraft (caused by the oxygen spillage), small stabilizing rocket motors were fired. It was then ascertained that, while the service module had been severely incapacitated, the command module was intact and in working order, as was the LM *Aquarius.* As matters developed, the equipment on the thin-walled, spider-like moon landing craft was brought into service to perform tasks for which it was not basically designed. The 31-second emergency firing of its engine, which would ordinarily have emanated from the service module, brought the craft into partial orbit around the moon. Another burst shortly afterward sent *Apollo 13* on its return journey — and corrected its course again when ground tracking disclosed that the craft was not on a true course. *Aquarius* provided water and oxygen for the men, and its battery provided the necessary power.

Apollo 14, which blasted off on its spectacular journey on January 31, 1971, carried Captain Alan B. Shepard, Jr., Commander Edgar D. Mitchell of the U. S. Navy, and Major Stuart A. Roosa of the U. S. Air Force.

What did Apollo 14 accomplish?

As the fifth and sixth men to set up scientific experiments on the lunar surface, astronauts Alan Shepard and Edgar Mitchell, in two separate walks that permitted them a rest period, hiked for more than three miles in the rugged Fra Mauro terrain. A specially designed cart helped in the collection of some 96 pounds of rocks and soil samplings, but hindered in the attempt to reach the top of Cone Crater as the astronauts clambered among giant boulders.

When *Apollo 15* was launched on July 26, 1971, it carried with it not only the usual three-man crew of astronauts, but a battery-powered car weighing about 460 pounds. In size and appearance it was reminiscent of a dune buggy. Each of its wheels was driven by a separate one-quarter horsepower motor. The vehicle, not unexpectedly, was dubbed the Lunar Rover.

What was the "Lunar Rover"?

Astronauts David R. Scott (who was the command module pilot for the ten-day earth-orbital flight of *Apollo 9,* a flight in which the lunar module was first flown), James B. Irwin (who had miraculously survived an airplane crash some ten years earlier), and Alfred M.

The Lunar Rover, first motorized vehicle to transport explorers on the moon.

A useful tool which facilitated the work of gathering lunar soil by U.S. astronauts was the lunar scoop. The tripod-like object also shown above (atop boulder in foreground) is the gnomon and photometric chart assembly used to establish sun angle, scale and lunar color.

What were the rewards of Apollo 15?

Not surprisingly, three separate motorized trips by the *Apollo 15* astronauts along the foothills of Mount Hadley, the edge of Hadley Rille, and across Hadley Plain yielded a scientific bounty in the form of about 168 pounds of moon samples. A television camera aboard the roving vehicle permitted viewers on earth to share with the explorers a spectacular and truly awesome moonscape. Amazing discoveries were also shared, as, for example, the multi-layered lunar soil in evidence along a terraced Hadley Rille. The first deep-drill cores taken on the moon, reaching eight feet in one operation, disclosed as many as 58 layers. Each layer, by itself, has a story of its own to tell, depicting an era in the moon's chronology.

Following the *Apollo 15* visit, seismic data transmitted to earth revealed a source of moonquakes west of Tycho Crater perhaps some 500 miles below the surface. There was conjecture that molten lava dozens of miles in diameter could be trapped in a pocket at that under-surface point, creating the moonquakes.

Visual observations and extensive photographic mapping of the moon were carried out by Alfred Worden in the orbiting ship. He also launched a subsatellite weighing 78 pounds which gathered and transmitted supplemental data to earth long after the astronauts returned from their mission. From 69 miles above the surface Worden viewed and reported volcanic cinder cones in the southeastern rim of the Sea of Serenity.

Worden (a "space rookie") were assigned to the mission. Scott and Irwin together took the landing craft *Falcon* to its descent over the Apennine Mountains while Worden whirled in lunar orbit. The landing site was near a meandering canyon known as Hadley Rille.

With improved equipment designed to lengthen man's stay on the lunar surface, Scott and Irwin were able to remain for more than 66 hours. Their explorations outside the lunar module alone occupied more than 18 hours, a time period that was nearly double that of the *Apollo 14* moonmen. More significantly, compared with a two-wheeled cart used in the previous mission to gather lunar specimens, the versatile Lunar Rover enabled Scott and Irwin to carry a greater variety and amount of material for scientific evaluation and to travel farther afield (a distance totaling about 17½ miles).

An immense split lunar boulder effectively dwarfs scientist-astronaut Harrison H. Schmitt at the Taurus-Littrow site on the moon.

John W. Young, Charles M. Duke, Jr., and Thomas K. Mattingly II were the men selected to complete *Apollo 16's* mission. They blasted off on April 16, 1972. Their destination: the Descartes Highlands, a region that seemed to correspond in many respects with the features to be found on the hidden side of the moon. As with the previous *Apollo* flight, a Lunar Rover was taken along to provide surface transportation.

What was Apollo 16's destination?

Astronauts John Young and Charles Duke spent 73 hours on the moon, 20¼ hours of which was spent outside the lunar module setting up instruments, exploring, and gathering samples. There were parallel major objectives to the *Apollo 15* mission, but these explorers were in the Sea of Rains. Again, the Lunar Rover served the astronauts well. It was driven approximately 17 miles upon very rugged terrain. A visit to the rim of Plum Crater (formed by meteorite impact) yielded rocks of potential importance.

210 pounds of lunar rocks and soil were brought to earth for examination and analysis by the crew of *Apollo 16*. Of the more than 30 soil samples collected, most were analyzed for carbon content. Simple organic compounds were present in these and earlier samples — which is not to conclude that these substances originated with life. Nonetheless, extensive analysis and scientific deduction can lead to information on how life might originate.

Apollo 17 marked the end of an era in the U.S. space program. Its crew was made up of Eugene A. Cernan, Ronald E. Evans, and Harrison H. Schmitt. Schmitt, who accompanied Eugene Cernan on the moon, was the first professional scientist to take part in the long journey and explore the lunar sur-

What were the goals of the last Apollo mission?

face. His credentials were impressive: he held a doctorate in geology from Harvard, a science degree from the California Institute of Technology, and in the course of his lifetime of geological training and research had helped train earlier astronauts for their required chores on the moon.

The last landing of the *Apollo* series was a smooth one as the lunar craft *Challenger* set down among craters and huge boulders near the southeast rim of the Sea of Serenity. The craft came to rest in a narrow valley, nestled between a 5,000-foot mountain to the north and a 7,000-foot mountain to the south. The date was December 11, 1972. Because of the adjacent Taurus Mountains and Littrow Crater, the landing site became known as Taurus-Littrow. Tranquility Base, site of the first manned landing by *Apollo 11,* was approximately 450 miles to the south.

Once again a Lunar Rover was assembled and operated by astronauts Cernan and Schmitt. It was a "new and improved" model, rigged to measure surface electrical properties and to record lunar gravity. A total of 23 miles was logged on the moon-rover vehicle in three separate traverses on the moon. At one point the astronauts were 4.7 miles from *Challenger,* the farthest distance any moonmen had ever gone from their lunar module base.

The basic goal of *Apollo 17* was to try to add missing links to the chain of information already received from earlier missions and surveys. To accomplish this, new instrumentation was brought along and more sophisticated experiments were devised. The astronauts had a variety of scientific tools to probe the moon's depths, measure gravity patterns or "waves," take the moon's pulse by recording moonquakes, and analyze atmospheric gases.

On the orbiting *America,* Ronald Evans was kept busy with many active experiments, including infrared photography to log temperature variations on the moon's surface, charting subsurface rock formations to a depth of almost a mile by means of radar, and mapping the moon in different ways.

What was assumed at the time to be a highly significant discovery by *Apollo 17's* men on the moon was some orange soil. It was thought that this could be oxidized iron associated with volcanic activity, but subsequent tests disclosed that the color was due to glass, not iron. Further, since the age of the soil was calculated to be approximately 3.8 billion years, it could not be tied in with more "recent" volcanic activity.

What has been learned through the Apollo program?

With the safe splashdown of *Apollo 17* on December 19, 1972, the moon-landing phase of an unprecedented space program lasting three and a half years was terminated. But it can be regarded in many ways as merely the end of the beginning. Sorting, cataloging, examining, assessing and reassessing the wealth of data may well keep scientists busy for decades to come. Of the 840 pounds of lunar material brought to earth, for example, only a fraction has been fully analyzed. Putting together the many pieces of a vast cosmic jigsaw puzzle takes time.

A great many suppositions and theories relating to the moon have been dispelled since closer inspection of its properties has been made possible. Yet, since it has been discovered also that the moon is a highly complicated mass with more bewildering features and characteristics than had been anticipated at the outset, there are still no easy answers to many questions. In some instances, more mysteries have arisen that conflict with various theories than have been laid to rest. The result is that there is still much scientific controversy as to the birth of the moon and its history, and, in a larger sense, to its relationship with our solar system.

These are some of the particulars drawn from the newly acquired fund of knowledge that are generally, if not absolutely, conceded:

Though there's no overall agreement on just where the moon came from, it seems fairly certain that it did not simply catapult into space (and orbit) from the fundamental earth-sphere. Nor could it have been a twin of the earth at birth. The moon has a low density, attributable to the near-absence of iron, while the earth, of course, has considerable iron. The distinctive composition of the moon cannot be likened to the composition of the earth, and there is no way to explain at the present time how such a disparate concentration of iron could exist in one twin of a pair. An interesting sidelight of this revelation is that the moon, indeed, is low in iron compared with the nucleus of our solar system, the sun. It does not even seem likely, therefore, that the moon was formed from the material of our nebula and captured by the earth. Perhaps (some scientists suggest) the moon was formed by means of a Saturn-like ring condensed from a silicate substance that girded the growing earth-mass like our present atmosphere. In such an event, we can say that the moon came into being from the earth, but indirectly — and more precisely — from its embryo.

Scientists continue to search for life or its remnants wherever they can probe within our solar system. The samples from the moon, subjected to life-detection methods, have yielded no life-forms whatsoever. Conclusion: there is no life on the moon, and there probably never was.

The moon appears to be without any water at all. Under such bone-dry circumstances, life as we know it is not possible. Indications are that the lunar rocks cooled without water.

The moon was apparently formed about 4.6 billion years ago. Some scientists believe that our solar system came into being at the same time; some believe that this event occurred several hundred million years earlier. The moon's early history was turbulent and volcanic, as that of the earth. But the lava plains, such as the Sea of Tranquility, where the first moonmen stepped forth, are many hundreds of millions of years younger than the moon. The craters into which lava flowed, some scientists say, were created by solid cosmic masses in collision, forming, at least in part, the base material of the moon. Cooled lava chunks brought back by *Apollo 11* have been dated at about 4 billion years. They might well have been

The Lunar Roving Vehicle, visible at left, brought Harrison Schmitt (shown in picture) to the site of a gigantic boulder.

The "orange soil" discovered during the *Apollo 17*'s extravehicular activity was thought at first to be oxidized iron, but it was glass.

part of the molten rock thrown thousands of miles when the moon sustained its most tremendous impact and the Sea of Rains was formed.

Lava flows, extensive meteoroid and asteroid bombardment, and rapid surface cooling between impacts continued until about 3 billion years ago, then ceased suddenly. The earth may have been subjected to the same cosmic violence at the time, but the evidence has been shattered, buried, changed by wind and water, heat and cold, and homogenized in the form of new mountains.

The moon has been "dead" geologically for about 3 billion years. Meteorites still shower upon it, but in fewer number. A huge meteorite excavated the crater known as Tycho about a billion years ago. About 900 million years ago, the crater Copernicus was formed by impact with another gigantic object.

Molten lava solidified on the moon at different times, forming several layers, or strata. Two main types of rock have been collected: basalt and breccia. Basalt is the most common type of volcanic rock. Breccia is made of soil and pieces of rock squeezed together by impact.

Much has been learned about the moon; but many mysteries still remain to be solved. And the mysteries can only be solved through scientific exploration. The manned flights of the *Apollo* series have ended, but lunar exploration in the future may be accomplished by such means as the *Lunokhod* vehicles developed by the Soviet Union. Visitations in one form or another, measurements, and observations will continue to take place, because the scientific thirst for knowledge cannot be quenched.

What of future moon exploration?

THE HOW AND WHY WONDER BOOK OF

PLANETS AND INTERPLANETARY TRAVEL

Written by
DR. HAROLD J. HIGHLAND
Associate Professor,
Chairman of the Department
of Business Administration,
College of Business Administration,
Long Island University

Illustrated by
DENNY McMAINS

Editorial Production:
DONALD D. WOLF

Edited under the supervision of
Dr. Paul E. Blackwood
Washington, D. C.

Text and illustrations approved by
Oakes A. White
Brooklyn Children's Museum
Brooklyn, New York

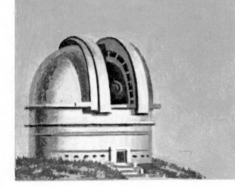

GROSSET & DUNLAP · Publishers · NEW YORK

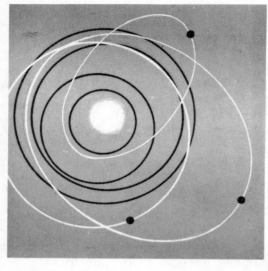

Introduction

When Neil A. Armstrong extended his left foot and formed the first footprint of a man on the brownish-gray powdery surface of the moon, he said, "That's one small step for a man, one giant leap for mankind." It marked the attainment of a long-sought goal. But now the moon itself is already being looked upon as but a steppingstone. Now the planets beckon. Scientists have set new goals to expand still further our knowledge of space.

Successes in space exploration are based on the proper application of scientific facts and principles relating to the laws of motion, the mechanics of flight, outer atmosphere, the planets and our solar system, and rocket fuels. *The How and Why Wonder Book of Planets and Interplanetary Travel* deals with many such facts and principles in an easy-to-understand way. Future flights into space will build on this knowledge and thus add new knowledge.

This intriguing book also explores the problems faced by scientists as they try to accomplish man's age-old dream of probing outer space. Can we use nuclear power for rocket fuel? How can we navigate a spaceship? Why are spaceships needed? Can man live on the moon? Answers to these and a multitude of other questions bring the reader up-to-date on space information. At the same time, further questions are propounded — ones for which scientists still seek answers. Thus is curiosity stimulated, and the work of science goes on.

If you are a hopeful candidate for a rocket trip, or merely an armchair observer of such events, you will find *The How and Why Wonder Book of Planets and Interplanetary Travel* a significant reading experience.

Paul E. Blackwood

Dr. Blackwood is a professional employee in the U. S. Office of Education. This book was edited by him in his private capacity and no official support or endorsement by the Office of Education is intended or should be inferred.

Contents

ANDROMEDA

MILKY WAY

SOLAR SYSTEM

Shaping the Space-Age Dream

Man has always looked for new lands,

Why should we explore space?

new mountains, new worlds to conquer. For some, there was a practical reason, such as searching for gold, or for an even more precious commodity — freedom. For

others, there was the adventure and romance of being the first man to fly across the ocean or the first man to explore an unknown cave.

Ever since early history, man has been curious. First, he explored his cave, then the land, next the sea and

4

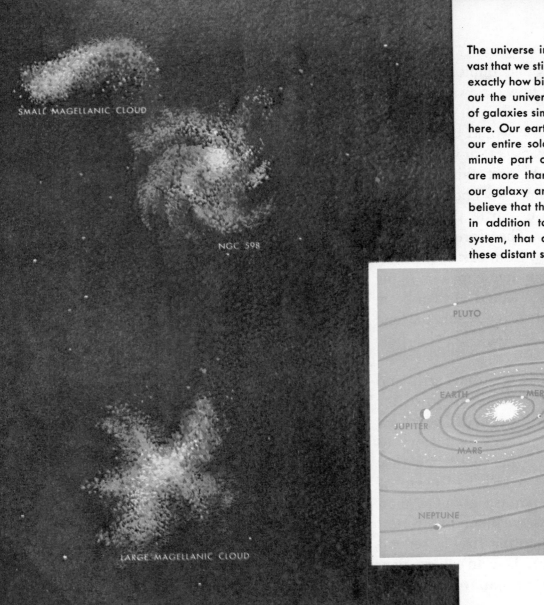

SMALL MAGELLANIC CLOUD

NGC 598

LARGE MAGELLANIC CLOUD

The universe in which we live is so vast that we still have not discovered exactly how big it really is. Throughout the universe there are millions of galaxies similar to the one shown here. Our earth and sun — in fact, our entire solar system — is but a minute part of our galaxy. There are more than 100 billion stars in our galaxy and many astronomers believe that there are other planets, in addition to those in our solar system, that are revolving around these distant suns.

PLUTO

SATURN

EARTH

MERCURY

JUPITER

VENUS

ASTEROIDS

MARS

URANUS

NEPTUNE

eventually the air. Today, man stands at a new frontier — space and space travel.

As we go up into the air over the earth, **What is space?** we will not find any road sign along the way saying, "You are now entering space." Actually, once we leave the ground we are in space. The airplanes that fly overhead are in space. But they are only at the very bottom of space. Today, man is interested in *outer space*.

Although scientists have not agreed upon where outer space begins, there are many who feel that once we are about 600 miles above the earth, we are at the bottom fringe of outer space. If this is the bottom, where is the top?

The top or farthest reaches of outer

space is millions and millions of miles away. No matter how far away from the earth we go, we would still be in outer space. In effect, we would be traveling through the universe (U-ni-verse). The universe is the biggest thing we can picture. Everything we know of is in the universe — our earth, the sun, the very distant stars. Therefore, no matter how far out we go from earth, either by exploring with our telescopes or flying in a spaceship, we would always be in the universe and never reach the end of outer space.

The dream of leaving the earth and

When did man first dream of space travel?

reaching another world can be traced back in history to the second century A.D. At that time a Greek, Lucian of Samos, wrote a fantasy about a man who was carried to the moon by a waterspout during a storm. In his second story about space, Lucian's hero flew to the moon with a pair of wings he had made himself.

The moon was the obvious destination for such fantasies because it is so large and has clearly visible markings, which could be thought of as land and sea areas. But for the next 1,400 years, the dream of reaching the moon was abandoned. During this period men believed that the earth was the only world that had ever been created, and that the sun, moon and stars were there to give light and comfort to the earth.

It was not until some 300 years ago, when the famous Italian astronomer Galileo looked through his telescope and told about the other worlds he saw,

that men realized there were other worlds in addition to our earth. Again, they began to dream of reaching these worlds.

In 1634, there appeared a story about a journey to the moon by Johannes Kepler, the German astronomer who discovered how the planets moved about the sun. Although Kepler was a scientist, he transported his hero to the moon by "magic moon people" who could fly through space. Kepler did include a detailed description of the surface of the moon, which he had seen through his telescope.

After Kepler's book, there were many others about space travel and voyages to the moon. They were mostly fantasies, but some contained attempts at scientific reasoning. The first serious discussion of space travel was written in 1640 by Bishop Wilkins of England. It contained a description of physical conditions on the moon and discussed ways in which man could possibly live on the moon. The first man who wrote about a rocket as a spaceship was the noted Frenchman, Cyrano de Bergerac. In his *Voyage to the Moon* and *History of the Republic of the Sun,* he had his space travelers flying to the moon and the sun inside a rocket.

When these books were written about 300 years ago, no one seriously thought that it would be possible to fly through space. It was not until Jules Verne, the French novelist, wrote his story *From the Earth to the Moon* in 1865 that any attempt was made to apply known scientific principles to the space vehicle. By the time that H. G. Wells, the English author, wrote *The First Men on the*

The ancient Egyptians believed their valley was the universe.

Moon in 1901, man was already at the beginning of a new era in the development of air travel and the conquest of space.

The Earth and Its Atmosphere

The *atmosphere* (AT-mos-phere) is a mixture of gases that surrounds the earth. It is composed of oxygen, nitrogen, carbon dioxide and other gases. Scientists have divided the atmosphere into four layers or levels. Closest to the earth, up to a height of about 10 miles, is the *troposphere* (TROP-o-sphere). This layer contains nine-tenths of all the air surrounding the earth. It is in this layer that our clouds are formed and our weather is made.

What is the atmosphere?

The second layer, the *stratosphere* (STRAT-o-sphere), which starts 10 miles up and extends to about 50 miles, contains much less air than the troposphere. Here it is very difficult to breathe, since there is very little oxygen. Above this layer is the ionosphere (i-ON-o-sphere), which extends between 250 and 300 miles above the earth. In this layer there is very little air, and it would be impossible for man to live there for a few minutes without extra oxygen needed for breathing. Furthermore, the sky from this altitude appears black, even though the sun is shining.

In the second century A.D., the Greek astronomer Ptolemy believed the sun and planets revolved around the earth.

Galileo built his first telescope in Italy in 1610.

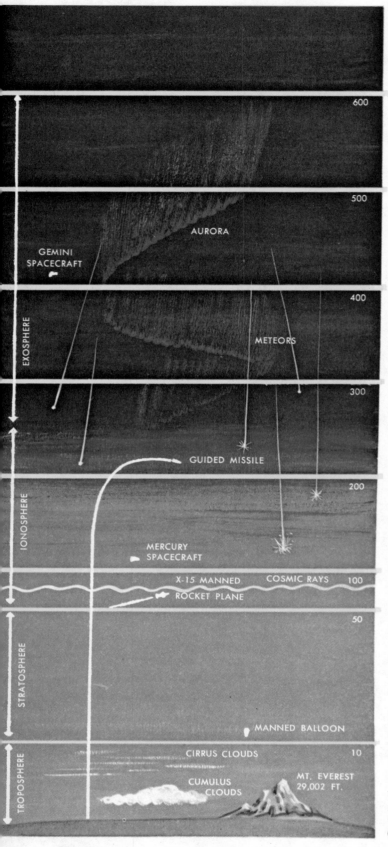

The air between earth and outer space is the atmosphere.

Finally, at 600 miles up and beyond to the far reaches of the universe is the exosphere (EX-o-sphere). This layer contains practically no gases or air and is very, very dark. The exosphere extends out beyond the moon, sun and distant stars.

Man has been probing space ever since

How have we probed the near-reaches of space?

he first turned his eyes skyward to observe the sun, moon and stars. It was not until 1610, however, when Galileo developed his telescope, that man really began to explore beyond the earth. While the telescope provided much information about the heavens, it is only recently that we have obtained detailed information about the space surrounding the earth.

We gathered this information in many ways. First, astronomers used the spectroscope (SPEC-tro-scope) with their telescopes to determine the composition of the stars. The spectroscope is an instrument which uses a prism to separate light rays into their colors. Every element in nature emits a special combination of colors when very hot. The combination for each element is as distinctive as a fingerprint. Each star, like our sun, is very hot and emits rays of light. Therefore, by analyzing these color combinations, it was possible to determine the substances which exist in the stars.

Radio telescopes have provided us with more information than the large 200-inch telescope at Mount Palomar, California. To use a radio telescope, we send radio signals into space, aiming at

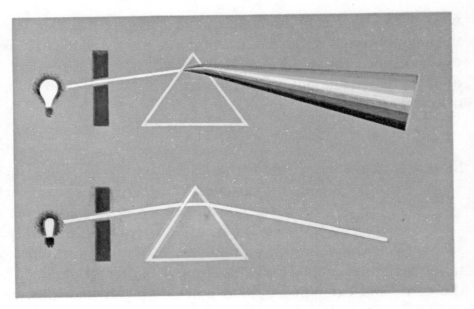

The light from our sun or an ordinary lamp, when it passes through a prism, is refracted (broken up) into an array of colors like a rainbow. But when light from a lamp filled with a single chemical passes through a prism, only the color emitted (given off by the chemical in the bulb) passes through the prism and is not refracted. Astronomers, by studying these light arrays, or spectrums, can determine what chemicals exist in the stars far away from earth.

some part of the sky. These waves bounce back from any object in the sky, such as the moon or a star, in the same way as a ball bounces back to you when you throw it against a wall. The telescope picks up these waves, and scientists, by studying the time it took the waves for their entire trip, can plot surface maps of the heavenly bodies.

Orbiting manned space vehicles in the *Mercury, Gemini,* and *Apollo* series have significantly extended man's knowledge in this field. Astronauts' visits to the moon have also provided additional information.

Scientific satellites sent into orbit around the earth — such as *Explorer, Pegasus* and *Nimbus* — have provided new and valuable information on phenomena of the upper atmosphere. Soon, new and more versatile spacecraft, like *Viking,* will land on Mars to send back valuable information about that planet. Scientists also hope to send a *Large Space Telescope* far beyond the earth's atmosphere to make accurate observation of the planets.

What are cosmic rays? Our sun is a massive, intensely hot body that is composed mainly of two gases — helium and hydrogen. Inside the sun these gases are pressed together under great pressure. The pressure is so great that the atoms, or basic chemical elements in the helium and hydrogen gases, are crushed together.

This crushing together of the atoms results in a tremendous release of energy, which is given off as heat, light and other rays. Cosmic rays are one of these other rays and they travel at a very, very high speed. These rays spread out from the sun in all directions and some reach the earth.

What is the danger of cosmic rays? Exposure to a large amount of cosmic rays would result in severe burns or even death. These rays destroy body tissue and the blood cells in our bodies. Fortunately, only a small portion of these rays reach us here on earth. Many of these rays are trapped thousands of

miles above the earth; an inconsequential amount comes through to us. Going out into space, though, we are exposed to an increased amount of cosmic rays, or cosmic radiation.

What are Van Allen belts? Satellites have confirmed the fact that the earth is surrounded by a huge swarm of high-speed, electrically charged atomic particles, beginning about 2,000 miles from the earth and extending 50,000 miles out into space. These particles form a huge doughnut-shaped belt, with the earth at the center of the "doughnut." This belt, known as the Van Allen radiation belt, was named after its discoverer, Dr. James Van Allen. No one knows where all the thousands of billions of particles come from, but most of them come from the sun. The orbital flights of American and Soviet astronauts have been well below the innermost boundary of the Van Allen belt. However, the radiation can be a danger to humans during the first hours of journeys to the moon and planets. The walls of today's spacecraft give partial protection to astronauts, and scientists are working on ways to eliminate the danger of radiation.

Every so often, giant eruptions, called flares, shoot out from the surface of the sun, flinging vast numbers of atomic particles toward the earth. These storms of particles would endanger the lives of astronauts, should they lack proper protection. Scientists are trying to learn how to predict solar flares so that an astronaut outside of his spacecraft, perhaps exploring the surface of the moon or "walking" in space, may be warned to return to safety.

What is space debris? Traveling at high speed throughout the universe are pieces of metal (mostly iron and nickel) and rock called *meteoroids* (MEE-tee-or-oids) by astronomers. Only about two of every thousand meteoroids are larger than a grain of sand. Most are probably no larger than this letter "o." A very few range from the size of a pebble to the size of a bus. The big meteoroids may weigh more than a hundred tons. (Astronomers also call meteoroids *space debris*.)

About 8 billion meteoroids, traveling at speeds up to 160,000 miles per hour, enter the earth's atmosphere every day. Within it they are called *meteors*. Speeding through our atmosphere, they strike atoms of air and create enough heat to burn up. Rarely, a large meteor may pass through the atmosphere and strike the earth. Those that do are called *meteorites*.

Any meteoroid that strikes a spacecraft is also called a meteorite. A sand-grain-sized meteoroid vaporizes, burning a tiny pit in a spacecraft's outer wall. A pebble-sized meteoroid would punch a hole through a spacecraft, and a large one would entirely demolish the craft.

Nevertheless, scientists feel that a spaceship will not have any difficulty with meteoroids. There is only about one chance in ten thousand that a craft in flight from the earth to the moon would encounter a meteoroid large enough to penetrate an eighth-of-an-inch steel skin of a spaceship. Then, if the ship had several layers of "skin," the chances of any danger from meteorites would be far less.

Casings and fragments of hardware from rockets that have orbited satellites or manned space capsules, as well as satellites that are no longer working, comprise thousands of pieces of space debris now orbiting the earth.

The Worlds Beyond Our World

What is the solar system? The heavenly body with which we are most familiar is the earth. It is one of the nine major planets that revolve about the sun. A *planet* (PLAN-et) is a heavenly body which revolves about a sun. It shines not because of its own light but by the reflection of light from the sun. For example, if you took a lighted electric bulb, it could resemble our sun. Then if you placed a mirror-surfaced ball near it, you would see that the ball was lighted. Actually, the ball is only reflecting the light from the electric bulb.

In addition to the planets there are perhaps 100,000 *planetoids* (PLAN-et-oids), also called *minor planets* or *asteroids* (AS-ter-oids). They differ from the major planets, such as the earth, mainly in size. The largest of these is Ceres, which has a diameter of about 480 miles or about the same size as the state of Texas. Most of the asteroids are small, only about a few miles across, and some are only two feet in diameter.

The next most familiar heavenly body to us is our moon. It is a *satellite* (SAT-el-lite) or a heavenly body that revolves around a larger one in much the same way that the earth is a satellite of the sun. Six of the nine major planets have one or more satellites, or moons, revolving around them. While the earth has only one moon, the planet Jupiter has twelve.

Also traveling around the sun are a number of *comets* (COM-ets). The typical comet has a head and a tail. The head consists of a mixture of gases and small solid particles similar to meteorites. The tail is comprised of many gases. The comet glows as it moves through the heavens.

Many of the comets revolve around the sun in the same manner as the planets, while others come from some distance away in the universe, pass around the sun and then disappear.

Together, the major planets, their satellites, the asteroids, comets, meteorites and our sun form the solar system.

This solar system together with the billions of stars that surround it form our *galaxy* (GAL-ax-y). The galaxy in which we live is called the Milky Way. If we join our galaxy with all the other many billions of galaxies, we then have the universe.

same is true of the sun and earth even though there is no string between them. As the earth and the other planets travel around the sun, they are pulling away from the sun. However, there is another force that is "pulling" on the earth — that is gravity (GRAV-i-ty).

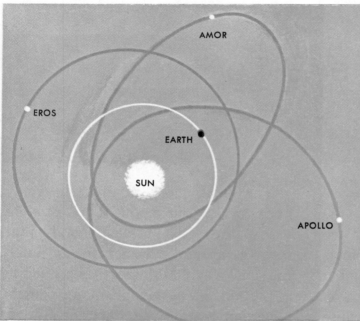

The asteroids that lie between the orbits of Mars and Jupiter revolve about the sun in elliptical orbits just as the planets in our solar system do.

Why do the planets revolve about the sun?

If you were able to stand in space millions of miles above the North Pole and observe our solar system, you would find all the planets circling about the sun in a counterclockwise direction, like the hands of a clock running backwards. Why do the planets follow this pattern? If you've ever flown a model airplane in a circle, while holding it with a string, you already know the answer. If you take a model airplane tied to a string, and let it fly in a circle around you, you will find that as long as the airplane travels at the same speed, it stays in the same path and it stays the same distance from you. The

There are nine planets, including the earth, revolving about the sun.

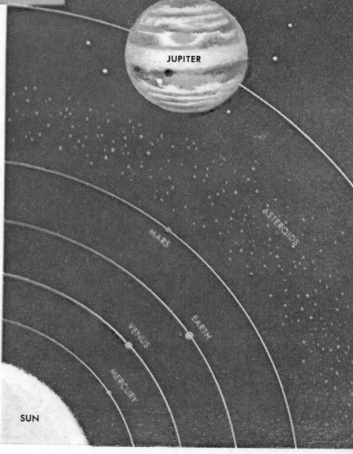

The sun's gravity pulls on the earth and the planets in the same way that the earth's gravity pulls on you. All bodies in the universe have a gravitational attraction on each other.

Gravity is forever exerting its pull. If

How does gravity work?

you throw a ball into the air, it falls to earth because of the pull of gravity. In the seventeenth

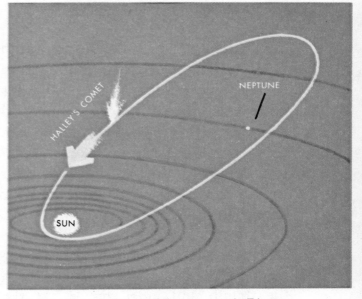

Halley's comet orbits around the sun once in 76 years and it will be visible over the earth in 1986.

century, Sir Isaac Newton of England discovered what we call the "laws" of gravity. He found that all bodies in the universe have an attraction power, and that the power force of gravity depends upon several things. First, the greater the amount of matter or weight of a body, the greater is its gravity pull. For example, the earth has a greater gravitational pull than the moon, just as the sun has a greater gravitational pull than the earth. Second, Newton found that the distance between the bodies affects the strength of this force. Thus, gravity has a stronger pull when the two bodies are closer together than when they are farther apart.

Did you ever spin a top or a gyroscope?

How does rotation differ from revolution?

As the top or gyroscope turns round and round rapidly, it is rotating (RO-TA-ting). Astronomers know that all the planets, including the earth, rotate around their own axis, or an imaginary line drawn through the center of the earth from the North Pole to the South Pole. It is this rotating motion that causes night and day. As the earth spins on its axis, part of it faces the sun and the other part faces away from the sun. One complete rotation takes twenty-four hours or a day. At times, we refer to half a rotation as daytime and the other half as nighttime.

This rotating motion is called *sidereal* (si-DE-re-al) motion by astronomers. Hold a ball in your hand between the thumb and index finger. At the point where the thumb touches the ball, picture the South Pole, and where the index finger touches the ball, the North Pole. Put a chalk mark halfway between the poles. This will be the equator or middle of the earth. Now place another chalk mark near the North Pole. As you rotate the ball and make one complete turn, you will see that the mark at the equator has to travel a bigger distance than the mark near the pole. In other words, the mark at the equator has to travel faster than the mark near the pole since it covers a longer distance.

This is also true on earth. In New York and Chicago, for example, the earth's sidereal motion or speed amounts to 700 miles an hour or 12 miles a minute. At the same time that the earth is rotating, it is also moving around the sun. This movement is called *revolution* (rev-o-LU-tion). One complete trip around the sun is one revolution, or, as we know it, one year. To make this trip the earth travels at a speed of 18½ miles per second. In one hour it covers more than 66,600 miles in space on its orbital trip around the sun.

What is a planetary orbit? The planets revolve about the sun in a planetary orbit; that is, they move in an ellipse (el-LIPSE) or elongated circle. To draw an ellipse, stick two thumbtacks into a piece of cardboard about four inches apart. Make a loop of string about four inches long and slip it over the tacks. The loop should not be too taut. Stick a pencil point through the loop and stretch the loop out. Then, holding the

The earth's rotation results in day and night as parts of the earth face toward or away from the sun. The earth's revolving in an elliptical orbit about the sun results in the four seasons of the year.

NIGHT

300 MPH
700 MPH
OVER 1,000 MPH

DAY

SPRING
WINTER
583,765 MILES
SUN
93 MILLION MILES
18.5 M.P.S.
SUMMER
FALL

pencil in this fashion, move it along the string and draw on the cardboard. You have now drawn an ellipse.

The points where the thumbtacks are placed are called the focal points of the ellipse. It was the German astronomer Kepler who proved that the planets revolve about the sun in an elliptical or planetary orbit and that the sun is located at one of the focal points.

The earth, like the other planets, travels about the sun in an elliptical orbit. At its nearest point, or *perihelion* (per-i-HE-li-on), the earth is 91.4 million miles away from the sun. At its farthest point, or *aphelion* (a-PHE-li-on), the earth is 94.6 million miles from the sun. The average distance between the earth and sun, according to astronomers, is 93 million miles.

What is the asteroid belt? Between the orbits of the planet Mars and Jupiter is a space some 350 million miles wide. For many years, astronomers thought that there should be a planet in this space because

it was so large and it left a gap in what they considered the normal spacing between planets. In 1801, astronomers found a heavenly body only about 480 miles wide. They watched it through their telescopes and found that it revolved around the sun like a planet. Several years later they discovered many more "small planets" in this portion of the sky.

Today, we know this region as the asteroid belt. It is believed to include more than 100,000 planetoids or asteroids. Some are ball-shaped, like the earth, while others are like irregular chunks of rock. The largest of the asteroids is Ceres, 480 miles in diameter. Other known asteroids are much smaller. Adonis, Apollo and Hermes are only about a mile or less in diameter.

Between these asteroids and the sun are the *inner planets* — Mercury, Venus, Earth and Mars. The planets beyond the asteroids — Jupiter, Saturn, Uranus, Neptune and Pluto — are known as the *outer planets*. (See illustration, pages 12-13.)

The earth, like the other planets and asteroids, revolves about the sun in an elliptical orbit. You can draw these orbits of our solar system, using a pencil, two thumbtacks and a piece of string.

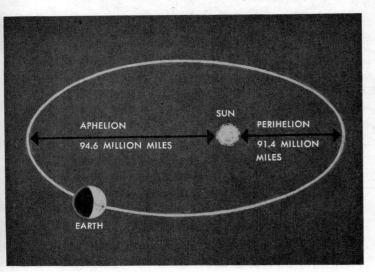

APHELION
94.6 MILLION MILES

SUN

PERIHELION
91.4 MILLION MILES

EARTH

Mercury, the nearest planet to the sun,

Why will it be difficult to explore Mercury? is also the smallest. It is only slightly larger than our moon — 3,100 miles in diameter as compared with our moon's 2,160 miles. Because of its small size, there is very little gravity as compared with earth. For example, if you weigh 100 pounds on earth, you would weigh only 35 pounds on Mercury.

MERCURY

EARTH

The pull of gravity is what holds the clouds and air around the earth. On Mercury, however, there is no atmosphere because the gravity is so low. Thus, there are no clouds, no rain, no water on that planet.

Mercury completes its orbit around the sun, or makes one full trip in its ellipse, in only 88 earth days. Mercury rotates on its axis very slowly. It does not keep the same face toward the sun, as astronomers thought until recently. Instead, it makes three rotations for every two revolutions around the sun. Here the temperature reaches almost 650° F. On its side away from the sun, the temperature drops to —260° F. At this very low temperature, it is so cold that oxygen (which we need for breathing) and nitrogen (which we have in our air) would be frozen solid.

The intense heat and extreme cold, the dangerous glare from the burning sun, the lack of water and the low gravity would make it most difficult to explore the surface of Mercury.

The hot sun shines down continually on one side of Mercury; here the heat is so intense that lead would boil.

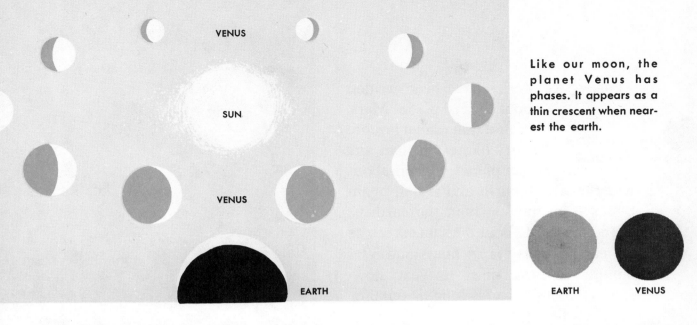

VENUS

SUN

VENUS

EARTH

Like our moon, the planet Venus has phases. It appears as a thin crescent when nearest the earth.

EARTH   VENUS

What will we find on the planet Venus?

Venus, about the same size as the earth, and often called "our sister planet," is also our nearest neighbor in space. At its nearest point, Venus is 26 million miles from earth. It is the brightest of all planets because of the reflection of the sun from its massive clouds. No one has ever seen the surface of Venus — even with the most powerful telescope — since the planet is always completely covered with thick white layers of clouds.

These clouds are not like those we have on earth, which are composed of water vapor, ice crystals and some dust. The clouds of Venus, according to astronomers, consist of large amounts of dust and crystals of frozen carbon dioxide.

The Venus clouds do not change their shape, and this has led scientists to conclude that there are no great oceans and land masses or continents on Venus, as there are on earth. If there were large oceans and land areas, vertical air currents would be formed similar to those on earth; and if these air currents were present, they would penetrate the cloud cover and cause the clouds to move.

In 1962, the United States space probe, *Mariner 2*, passed within 22,000 miles of Venus. Information radioed back to earth indicated that the surface temperature there was as high as 800° Fahrenheit. Russia's *Venus 4* space probe, in 1967, entered the atmosphere of Venus and parachuted instruments to the planet's surface. These measured the temperature of the atmosphere, finding it to range from 104° to 536° F. *Venus 4* also found that the Venusian atmosphere is almost pure carbon dioxide, a fact confirmed by the United States *Mariner 5* which swooped to 2,480 miles of the surface of Venus the day after *Venus 4* arrived.

Obviously, the surface of Venus is too hot to support life as we know it. *Mariner 2* had found that Venus rotates on its axis in the direction opposite that of the earth's rotation, the Venusian day being as long as 225 earth days. This probably results in winds that blow vast dust storms over Venus's hot, waterless surface. It will be a long time before men find a way to explore Venus.

Many space stories have been written about the red planet Mars, because that planet is more nearly like earth than any other planet. Mars is about half the size of earth and is half again as far from the sun than the earth is. Mars rotates at about the same speed as the earth. Its day is 24 hours and 37.4 minutes of earth time. Its year, however, is about twice as long as ours, or 686.7 earth days.

Is Mars another earth?

Because it is some 50 million miles farther from the sun than the earth, Mars receives less than half the light and heat from the sun than we do. Its temperature could be tolerated by a spaceman, since it is not too different from that on earth. Around the center of Mars, similar to the equator of earth, the daytime temperature rises to about 85° F., and at night, it drops to somewhat below freezing. At its polar regions, the temperature of Mars is slightly above freezing in the daytime, but it goes as low as −200° F. at night.

Because it is smaller than earth, its gravity is lower, only slighter greater than that which would be found on the planet Mercury. Another difference is its atmosphere. While it contains water vapor and carbon dioxide, there is no trace of pure oxygen gas, as there is in the earth's atmosphere.

The Martian landscape has fascinated men for centuries. Polar ice caps are visible during the winter season on Mars. During the summer, the ice caps appear to melt and the white surface of the ice disappears. In place of it we find a large green-looking area. Recent explorations of Mars with radio telescopes indicate that these polar caps are not like those on earth. Whereas the earth's polar caps are hundreds of feet thick, the Martian ice caps are about one-twenty-fifth of an inch thick.

The question of why the surface appears green has long puzzled scientists. How could life exist without oxygen in the air to breathe? This has been answered partially by plants we have on earth, lichens. These small plants produce their own oxygen in the daylight and use it at night instead of drawing it from the atmosphere. We do not know if these are the Martian plants or not, but it is believed they might be.

In addition, astronomers have observed large bright areas, reddish in color, which they thought to be deserts, and large dark areas, which they believed to be oceans. The consensus among scientists today is that the dark areas are a form of plant life similar to

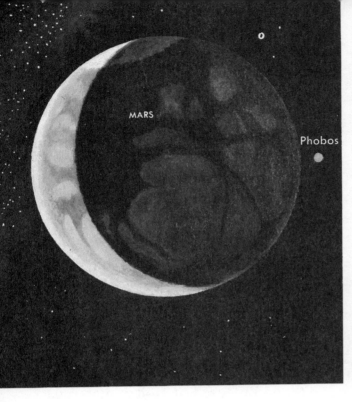

confirmed these findings and they also showed that much of the irregular terrain of Mars is caused by erosion. Photographs also showed what appeared to be dry river beds. Scientists now think that there may have been water and perhaps floods on Mars in the past.

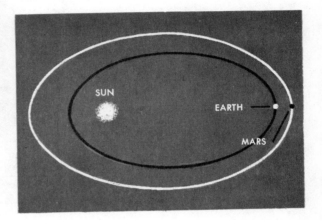

There are advantages in sending a rocket or spaceship to Venus before sending one to Mars. First, Venus is closer to the earth — some 26 million miles as compared with 35 million miles, which is the nearest Mars comes to earth. Second, the earth and Venus are in this close position every 19 months, whereas the earth and Mars are closest only once in 25 months. On the other hand, a space vehicle has to gain speed as it travels from earth to Venus. The earth's speed in orbit (sidereal rate) is 66,000 miles an hour as compared with 78,000 miles an hour for Venus. In a shot at Mars, the space vehicle has to reduce its speed, since Mars' orbital speed is only 54,000 miles an hour, or 12,000 miles slower than earth's orbital speed.

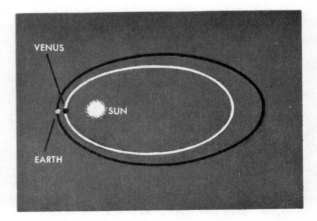

that which is visible at the polar regions during the summer. Scientists also believe that the bright areas are mineral or rock surfaces. One reason why many people believed that intelligent life existed on Mars is the presence of what seemed to be irrigation canals. In July, 1965, the U.S. space probe *Mariner 4* sped past Mars, only 7,400 miles from the planet's surface, and transmitted pictures back to earth. These pictures showed no water or artificial canals. The small area photographed did, however, reveal — meteor craters.

In August, 1969, *Mariner 6* and *Mariner 7* swooped toward Mars, approaching within a distance of about two thousand miles. While *Mariner 6* pictures again disclosed many craters and other features reminiscent of the lunar surface, the *Mariner 7* pictures gave a contrasting view. Scientific observers on earth saw many varied markings "totally unlike the moon in this gross scale."

Jupiter, the largest of all the planets,

What is the inner core of Jupiter like?

JUPITER

•
EARTH

has the shortest "day" as measured by earth time — 9 hours and 55 minutes. It shines brightly in the sky because it is so large, and it is about eleven times greater in size than the earth. There are thirteen moons that orbit around Jupiter in an elliptical pattern, just as the planets do around the sun. Four of the moons are as large as, or larger than, our own moon, which is 2,160 miles in diameter. Eight of Jupiter's moons vary in size from about 15 to 100 miles in diameter. The thirteenth, only recently discovered, is probably only three to five miles in diameter.

Several large gaseous layers of clouds surround the surface of Jupiter. Some are composed of poisonous ammonia and methane gases, and others consist of hydrogen and helium gases, like those of the sun. Within one of these large cloud layers is a giant red area — "the red spot of Jupiter," as astronomers call it. This red spot is somewhat larger than the earth and it was first seen in 1875. We do not know what makes it red, but we have noticed that it has

become fainter and fainter every year.

Circling the sun at a distance more than five times the distance from the sun to the earth, Jupiter receives very little light or heat from the sun. Its surface is believed to be a thick mass of ice that never melts. The surface temperature is about $-215°$ F.

For many years, Jupiter has been called a "gas giant," for it was impossible to determine whether or not it was really solid below the ice. Using radio telescopes, and observations by the *Pioneer 10* spacecraft, astronomers have now found that the inner core of Jupiter is composed of molten material, perhaps as hot as 54,000° F., more than six times the temperature of the sun's surface. How can the outside covering be solid ice when the inside is very hot? Wouldn't the heat melt the ice? But astronomers are sure of the ice covering and the hot molten material inside. What they do not know is what is in between. Some believe that there is an insulating material separating the hot material inside from the ice outside.

Jupiter, the largest and the fastest-rotating planet, completes one rotation in less than 10 earth hours.

ARTIST'S CONCEPTION OF JUPITER'S SURFACE

Others believe that there is a layer of water between the two. Other spacecraft may soon explore Jupiter's atmosphere and explain this mystery.

Because of its tremendous size, the gravity pull of the planet Jupiter is 2.64 times greater than that on earth. This means that a spaceman who weighed 200 pounds on earth would weigh 528 pounds on Jupiter. It also means that it would require much more power to blast off in a spaceship from Jupiter than it does from earth.

Saturn is similar to Jupiter in many ways. It, too, consists of a molten core that is surrounded by an ice cover thousands of miles thick. It also has an atmosphere filled with deadly methane and ammonia gases. However, this atmosphere

What lies beyond Saturn's rings?

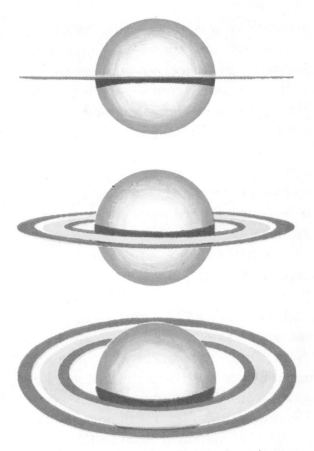

EARTH　　SATURN

The rings of Saturn, visible only through a telescope, appear at different angles each year. When they are tilted toward earth, Saturn's brightness increases.

is much more stable than Jupiter's; that is, it is more like our own sky on a calm, clear day as compared with our sky during a violent, windy thunderstorm.

Only slightly smaller than its sister "gas giant," Saturn is almost twice as far as Jupiter is from the sun. Saturn appears to radiate more heat than it receives from the sun. The surface temperature of the planet is about −285° F.

Like Jupiter, Saturn rotates quickly. Its day is equal to 10 hours and 12 min-

utes of earth time. Its year, or the length of one complete revolution around the sun, is about 29½ earth years.

There are two strange features about this planet. First, it has nine moons, the largest of which, Titan, is about the size of Mercury. But unlike the planet Mercury, Titan has a very small atmosphere. Furthermore, one of the moons of Saturn revolves from east to west, or clockwise, around the planet, while the other eight moons revolve in the normal solar system direction, counterclock-

Comparison in size of Saturn's moons with our moon.

TITAN

EARTH'S MOON

IAPETUS

RHEA

DIONE

TETHIS

PHOEBE　HYPERION　MIMAS　ENGELADUS

wise. Why this moon behaves in this manner, no one knows. It is one of the mysteries of astronomy and space.

The second strange feature about this planet is its rings. Imagine a grapefruit cut in half; one part is placed outside down on a very large plate and the other side is set against the bottom of the plate directly below the top half. This is the way the rings appear around Saturn.

Saturn's rings, which are much brighter than the planet itself, are composed of millions of small solid particles and ice crystals. The rings around the center of Saturn start at about 7,000 miles from the surface. There are several distinct rings and the farthest one away from the planet measures about 10 thousand miles in diameter. The whole ring system measures 170 thousand miles in diameter. Astronomers had believed that these rings were about 50 miles thick, but recent studies have put the thickness at only 10 miles.

The uncertainties about the planet and its great distance from the earth mean that no spaceship will reach Saturn until we have progressed far beyond our current technological levels in space travel.

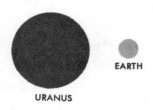

URANUS   EARTH

When first seen by astronomers in 1690,

Where is our sun only a brilliant star?

Uranus was thought to be a star. It was not until 1781 that Sir William Herschel of England discovered that Uranus was a planet that revolved about our sun just as the earth does. Uranus is twice as far as Saturn is from the sun or twenty times that of the earth from the sun. From that faraway distance, we believe that our sun looks like a bright star in the sky.

Unlike all the other planets, Uranus rotates on an imaginary axis that almost points directly at the sun. It would be much the same as if our earth were turned so that the North Pole would be almost pointing at the sun. In rotating on this axis, the north pole of Uranus faces the sun for almost twenty years. Then as the planet shifts, the rays of the sun move over the equator and shine over the south pole of Uranus for about

Uranus rotates strangely on its axis with the sun shining on the planet's north pole for 20 years. The planet then turns and its south pole faces the sun for 20 years.

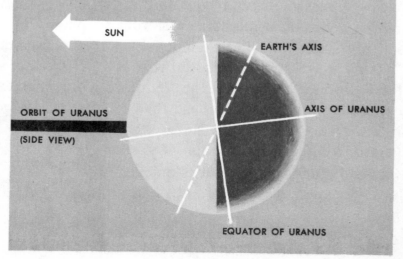

SUN

EARTH'S AXIS

ORBIT OF URANUS

(SIDE VIEW)

AXIS OF URANUS

EQUATOR OF URANUS

twenty years. Because of its great distance from the sun, little heat reaches that planet. The surface temperature is believed to be about −360° F.

Uranus is four times larger than the earth. It has a rocky core. It is not as dense or as heavy as the earth. Its surface gravity is slightly less than the gravity on earth. In addition, its atmosphere, or the gases surrounding the planet, are poisonous ammonia and methane.

EARTH

NEPTUNE

After Uranus was discovered, astrono-

How did gravity help astronomers discover Neptune?

mers were puzzled by its orbit around the sun. They knew that all heavenly bodies have a gravitational attraction or pull. Both the French astronomer Urbain Leverrier and the Englishman John C. Adams decided that there must be another planet beyond Uranus that was attracting it with its gravitational pull. Only in that way could the orbit of Uranus be explained. In 1848, the German astronomer Johann Galle located the new planet, Neptune, with his telescope exactly where Urbain Leverrier had predicted it would be.

Neptune is the outermost of the four "gas giants" and is more than three times larger than the earth. Its surface gravity is almost one-and-a-half times that of the earth — and is greater than any planet's surface gravity except Jupiter's. Like its sister "gas giants," it

Neptune, as it would be seen from one of its moons.

is covered with ammonia, methane, and possibly argon gas clouds over an icy surface. Astronomers believe that the temperature on Neptune's surface is about −375° F.

In some ways, Neptune and Uranus are more similar than the earth and Venus. The main difference between these two planets is that Neptune is somewhat colder and slightly smaller. It also appears bluish, while Uranus has a greenish hue when observed with a telescope. Little is known about the surface of either of these two distant planets, and we can only guess that the surface would be somewhat the same as that on Jupiter or Saturn.

After Neptune was discovered, astrono-

Why is Pluto called Planet X?

mers found that they still could not fully explain the orbit of Uranus. There had to be another heavenly body which was exerting a gravitational pull on Uranus so that it followed its strange orbit around the sun. A search was begun to find the missing planet. The letter X, used by mathematicians to signify an unknown quantity, was used as the name of the missing planet during the search.

PLUTO

EARTH

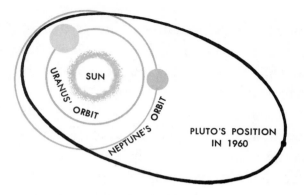

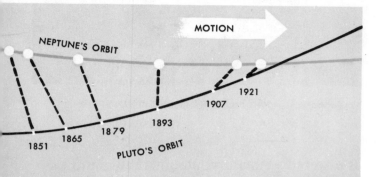

Both Pluto and Neptune revolve about the sun, but their orbits overlap and the planets cross each other twice in one complete revolution. A collision is possible, but it is thought unlikely since the nearest the two planets get to each other is 24 million miles.

In 1900, the American astronomer Percival Lowell started on his long search for Planet X. He directed much of the search and, finally, in 1930, the missing planet was found by Clyde Tombaugh. This planet was labeled "PL" for Percival Lowell and was called Pluto.

Pluto is more than 3½ billion miles from our sun. Its year, or one revolution around the sun, takes more than 248 earth years. It is somewhat larger than Mercury, and its interior is more like the earth's than its neighboring "gas giants." But there is still much we do not know about Pluto.

In studying Pluto, astronomers found that its orbit cut across Neptune's. Will they ever collide? Many years were spent to answer this question. It was found that the difference in speed at which these two planets revolve about the sun has prevented them from colliding thus far. It takes a considerable amount of mathematics to make these calculations. Maybe some day, millions of years from now, the two planets will collide. It can be computed mathematically if you have the years to work on the problem.

Because of the very large distances

How do astronomers measure distance?

they must measure in space, astronomers have developed special units of measure. In this way they can avoid using all those zeros, such as we encounter in measuring the distance of Pluto to the sun — 3,500,000,000 miles. One of the basic astronomical units is a *light year*.

Light travels at the speed of 186,000 miles per second. In one day a ray of light travels over 16,000,000,000 miles. In one year it travels 5,880,000,000,000 miles. To the astronomer, this is one light year.

So instead of writing this number with all the zeros, the astronomer merely writes "one light year."

The convenience of the light year unit

How far away are the stars?

of measure is readily seen when we start talking about distances to the stars. You have looked up into the sky at night and seen the stars. But what is a star? A star is a heavenly body that shines by its own light. That means it must be very hot to give off heat and light, just like our sun. Actually, our sun is a star; it is the nearest star to us — 93 million miles away.

Aside from our sun, how far is the nearest star? That star, called Proxima Centauri, is almost 25 trillion miles away. To the astronomer this is 4¼ light years.

The next nearest star is Alpha Centauri, and it is 500 billion miles farther away than Proxima Centauri. Alpha Centauri is in the constellation, or star group, known as *Centaurus,* and it has the same brightness as our sun. However, it is so far away that it appears as a mere dot in our sky.

What is a galaxy? A *galaxy* is a cluster, or group, of stars. Our solar system is part of such a group, or galaxy, in which there are more than 100 billion stars like our sun. The diameter of our galaxy is estimated to be 10 million light years, and remember that each light year is almost 6 million million miles.

Is there life on the other planets? More than a century ago, Joseph von Littrow, an astronomer in Vienna, suggested that we build many tremendous bonfires in the Sahara Desert in Africa. These fires would be a signal to any beings living on Mars. While the fires were never built, the speculation about life on Mars, on Venus and on the other planets has continued.

There are many people who believe that no intelligent, reasoning forms of life can exist in the choking atmosphere of Venus, or on the arid surfaces of Mars or, in fact, anywhere else in our solar system. Others, however, feel that life in some form may exist, but it would certainly be different from the life forms we know on earth. Thus far, there has been no definite proof to support the views of either side.

Early in 1961, scientists at the National Institute of Health in Washington, D. C. announced that they had started to grow "life" that they believed came from another world. These "bugs," as they called them, were little twisted rods about eight- to sixteen-millionths of an inch long. They found this "life" inside a meteorite that fell at Murray, Kentucky in 1950. This "life," according to the scientists, was unlike anything we have ever found on earth.

Our galaxy (our solar system and billions of stars) is a huge flat spiral about 475 million billion miles long. Below, a side view, and at the right, a top view. The cross indicates the position of our solar system.

Another group of scientists from Fordham University and Esso Research and Engineering Company in New York City announced at the same time that they, too, found "other-world life." They discovered waxy compounds inside a fragment of a meteorite that fell near Orgueil, France in 1864.

Although there are some scientists who feel that these two findings are now definite proof that life does exist elsewhere in the solar system, there are many others who do not accept these "proofs" of life. They feel that the waxy compounds are too similar to those we have on earth and that the meteorite became contaminated over the years, thus producing this strange substance. They also feel that the little twisted rods of life, which the Washington scientists presented, come from high up in our own atmosphere. Not until man is able to explore space more thoroughly and travel through it in his own spaceship, will he be able to obtain a definite answer about life on other planets.

Key to Planetary Exploration— the Spaceship

The Chinese used "war" rockets in A.D. 1232.

How did rockets spur space travel?
The exploration of space requires a special vehicle capable of very high speeds; that is, thousands of miles per hour. This space-exploring vehicle, or spaceship as we call it, is merely the next step after the giant rocket. Rockets have a long history of use for entertainment and war. Their greatest development came, however, when scientists realized that rocket power was needed to explore space and to enable spaceships to reach the moon and eventually the planets.

The earliest attempt to use rocket power to fly is supposed to have taken place more than 1,000 years ago in China. This early "spaceship" was a bamboo chair to which forty-seven rockets, or large firecrackers, similar to those shot into the air on the Fourth of July, were attached. The pilot of this early spaceship was a Chinese mandarin named Wanhu. When the firecrackers were ignited, the chair was supposed to shoot up into the air. Unfortunately, when they were ignited, Wanhu and his "ship" disappeared in a cloud of smoke and flame.

In their attack on Washington, D. C. in 1814, the English used a war rocket, which was invented by Sir William Congreve. The American Army was routed

"And the rockets' red glare, the bombs bursting in air . . ." was inspired by the British rocket bombardment of Fort McHenry in 1812.

and the British captured the capital. Several weeks later, these rockets were used during the British bombardment of Fort McHenry, near the city of Baltimore, Maryland. This famous event is referred to in the United States National Anthem, *The Star-Spangled Banner* — "And the rockets' red glare, the bombs bursting in air . . ." The rockets failed this time and Fort McHenry did not surrender.

It was not until early in the twentieth century that serious and extensive work in rockets began. An American physicist, Dr. Robert H. Goddard, built and fired working rockets that soared many miles into the air. He wrote a long article about how rockets could be used to explore the upper atmosphere, which balloons could not reach. He even suggested that a rocket could be fired to the moon. Though Goddard is now considered the "father of the modern

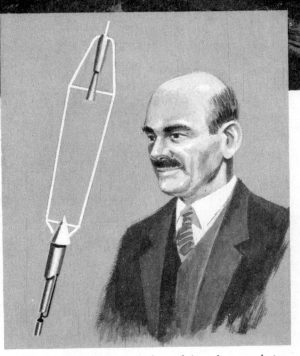

Dr. Robert H. Goddard, father of American rocketry, built and fired rockets more than forty years ago.

rocket," he was ridiculed for his ideas and his wonderful work was ignored in the United States.

In Europe, on the other hand, there were a number of scientists who recognized the value of Dr. Goddard's work. Among them was Dr. Werner von Braun, a key figure in the development of the deadly German V-2 rocket, which was used to bomb London during World War II. Von Braun's knowl-

The balloon flies like a rocket. As the air rushes out from the neck, the balloon shoots forward.

carried a smaller American-made rocket, the *WAC Corporal*. At the exact second when the V-2 rocket reached its fastest speed, the *WAC Corporal* started its own motor. Thus, it added to the speed it already had. The V-2 rocket dropped off when its fuel was consumed, and the *WAC Corporal* rocket continued going higher and higher. It reached a height of 250 miles above the earth before it started to come down.

FUEL

OXIDIZER

COMBUSTION CHAMBER

PUMPS

FUEL

COMBUSTION CHAMBER

AIR

SPARK

Two liquids, which are mixed and ignited in flight, are used to power a *liquid fuel* rocket.

The *ramjet*, simplest of all jet engines, has no moving parts and must be in motion before it will work.

edge and skill were used after the war by the United States in its rocket research and space programs at the Redstone Arsenal in Huntsville, Alabama.

The first true rocket-propelled space vehicle was fired on February 24, 1949. At that time, the United States Army sent up the first "two-stage" rocket at White Sands, New Mexico. They used a German V-2 rocket, which they had captured during World War II, and it

Why does a rocket fly?

Underlying the working of a rocket is a basic scientific rule — Newton's Third Law of Motion. It is named after Sir Isaac Newton, who was the first man to realize that these rules worked every time and everywhere in the world and even in the universe. Simply stated, this rule says that "for every action, there is an equal but opposite reaction."

Newton's third law explains why a rifle "kicks back" when it is fired. The action of the bullet moving forward out of the gun produces an equal force in the opposite direction. You can test this rule, or law, yourself. Take a balloon and blow it up. When you release it, it will zoom away from you. The balloon flies away because the air inside rushes out of the small opening

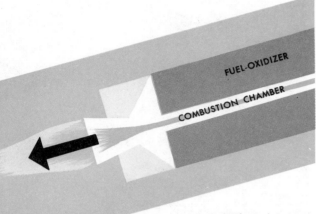

A *solid fuel* rocket uses several chemicals in powder or dough form for flight power.

in the back. In other words, the forward motion is an equal and opposite reaction of the air rushing out the back.

A rocket flies for the same reason. As hot gases, created by burning fuel, escape through the small opening in the rear of the rocket, they create an equal but opposite reaction which drives the rocket forward.

All of you have seen an airplane wing-

Can a rocket fly in outer space?

ing its way through the sky. It is able to do so because we have an atmosphere; that is, nitrogen, oxygen, argon, carbon dioxide and other gases which surround the earth in the troposphere and stratosphere. The airplane needs the air, which is forced over and under its wings by the propeller, or through its jet engines, in order to

help the plane rise and move forward. Without the atmosphere, the airplane would not be able to fly, and we know there is no atmosphere several hundred miles above the earth.

A rocket, on the other hand, because it works in accordance with Newton's Third Law of Motion, can operate more efficiently outside the atmosphere than within it. The atmosphere offers resistance, or pressure, against the forward moving rocket. You can test this resistance yourself on a windy day. Take a large piece of cardboard, about

Powerful rockets are used for space probes.

two or three feet square. If you hold it straight above your head and run into the wind, you will find that you feel a pressure against the cardboard; it may even pull your arms back somewhat. But if you hold the cardboard flat, so that only the thin edge faces the wind, you will find little resistance.

There is, however, a different problem which faces the rocket in space. To keep the rocket engine burning, there must be a supply of oxygen. There is oxygen, in gas form, in our atmosphere; it is the same oxygen that we breathe. In space there is no *free* oxygen, as scientists call it. Therefore, the rocket must carry its own supply.

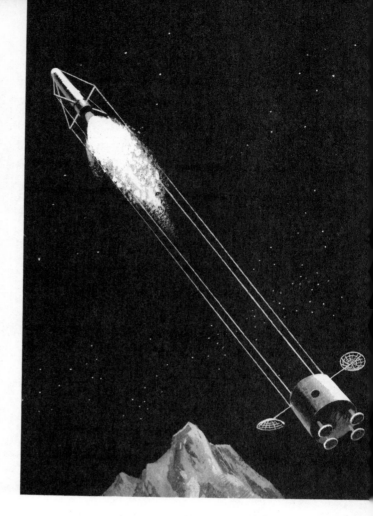

The rocket's thrust, or forward speed,

What fuel does a rocket use?

is created by the escape of hot gases through the rear openings or ports. These hot gases are created by burning fuel within the rocket. Basically, two types of fuel are used in rockets.

First, there is liquid fuel. This often consists of two liquids that are kept in separate tanks. When the two liquids are mixed and ignited, they vaporize or turn to gas. The gases expand when heated, and their only way to escape is through the rear openings. Two of

the liquids commonly used are alcohol and liquid oxygen. The liquid oxygen is called *LOX*. The oxygen is needed to support combustion or to enable the mixture to burn in space where no oxygen is available. Another liquid combination consists of high octane gasoline and nitric acid. The nitric acid contains oxygen which permits the mixture to burn.

Second, solid fuels are used in some rockets. This fuel consists of a mixture of several chemicals in powder form. One of the chemicals in the mixture must contain oxygen, which is released as a gas when it is heated. Without this release of oxygen, the mixture would stop burning much in the same way as a candle will stop burning if you cover it tightly by placing an inverted water

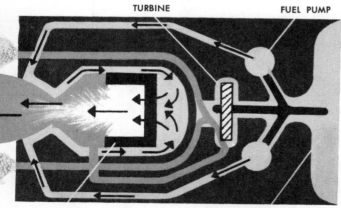

TURBINE   FUEL PUMP

REACTOR   FUEL (LIQUID HYDROGEN)

An atomic reactor and liquid hydrogen are used to power a *nuclear* rocket.

A nuclear-powered spaceship is today's dream of the space age. A nuclear motor is more efficient, developing greater thrust for its size than either liquid or solid fuel rockets. In plans for a nuclear-powered space trip to the moon, Mars or Venus, space engineers hope to use rockets to raise the spaceship above the earth's atmosphere. Here, the bottom stage would be detached and glide back to earth, while the smaller ship would speed ahead on its journey. The nuclear engine would be contained in front, and the men would travel in a gondola suspended by very long cables from the engine. In this way, the men would be better protected from the engine's radioactivity.

glass over it. The flame is snuffed out when its supply of oxygen is gone.

Governments and manufacturers of aerospace "hardware" have been experimenting with nuclear-powered, or atomic reactor, engines to replace the liquid and solid fuels used for rocket propulsion (the force needed to make a rocket move). In a nuclear-powered rocket, the motor consists of an atomic reactor through which liquid hydrogen is pumped. As the hydrogen is heated by the reactor, it turns into a gas and escapes through the rear ports of the rocket.

Can we use nuclear power for fuel?

A nuclear engine, though, generates extremely high temperatures — more than 6,300° F. — and so the motor section of a manned vehicle using such means would have to be well-insulated from the crew compartment. Considerable progress has already been made in designing such a device.

The speed necessary to overcome gravity is called *escape velocity*. When a rocket is launched on the earth, it is pushed upward according to Newton's law of motion. It is, however, encountering two other forces. One is the normal pull of the earth, or the earth's gravity. The other is the resistance of the atmosphere.

What is escape velocity?

31

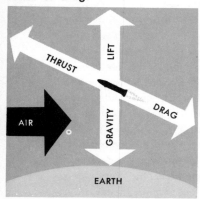

A space vehicle in our atmosphere is affected by four forces. Its *lift* must offset *gravity*; its forward *propulsion* must overcome air resistance or *drag*.

THRUST

LIFT

DRAG

AIR

GRAVITY

EARTH

EARTH

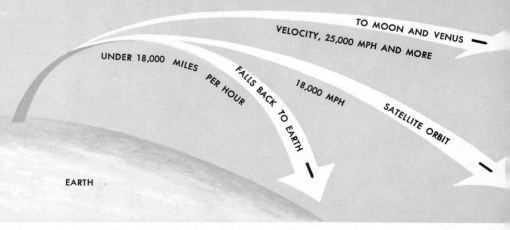

TO MOON AND VENUS

VELOCITY, 25,000 MPH AND MORE

UNDER 18,000 MILES PER HOUR

FALLS BACK TO EARTH

18,000 MPH

SATELLITE ORBIT

EARTH

At the speed of 18,000 miles per hour, the space vehicle's lift and propulsion are sufficient to keep it in orbit around the earth. To escape from the earth's gravitational pull, the vehicle must exceed 25,000 miles per hour.

Therefore, the rocket's forward thrust, or speed, must be high enough to overcome these two opposing forces.

A spaceship taking off from another planet or the moon would also encounter gravity, or the pull of that heavenly body. In some cases, there is also an atmosphere. Thus, the escape velocity problem exists elsewhere in space as it does on earth.

On earth, once the speed of 18,000 miles per hour is reached, it is sufficient to offset the pull of the earth, or the gravitational force. At that speed, however, the rocket, spaceship or satellite would remain at approximately the same fixed distance away from earth, circling it as the moon does. We call this going into orbit. The first successful orbital shot was made in October, 1957, when the Soviet Union placed its first satellite *Sputnik I* in orbit around the earth. In January, 1958, the American satellite *Explorer I* was fired into its globe-circling orbit.

If the rocket fails to reach a speed of approximately 18,000 miles an hour, it will not go into orbit, but will return to earth. The spaceship in which Russian cosmonaut Major Yuri Gagarin flew in

August, 1961, reached orbital speed. The Mercury capsules in which American astronauts Commander Shepard and Captain Grissom flew, traveled about 5,100 miles per hour. They did not go into orbit because the capsules had not reached orbital velocity.

To escape entirely from the earth's gravitational pull, it is necessary to attain a speed of about 25,000 miles per hour. At this speed, the rocket or spaceship would pull free of earth and head out into space. The United States' satellite *Pioneer IV* reached this high speed and left the earth's gravitational pull. Like the planets, it went into orbit around the sun.

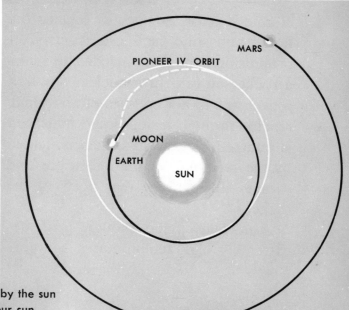

MARS

PIONEER IV ORBIT

MOON

EARTH

SUN

A rocket that misses the moon is attracted by the sun and goes into a planet-like orbit around our sun.

The Techniques of Flight

Who designed the modern spaceship? One of the earliest attempts at a practical rocketship was made by a Roumanian professor named Hermann Oberth. Because he wrote serious technical books about rockets and space travel during the days immediately after World War I, he was hired by a movie company to be technical adviser for a space-travel motion picture called "The Girl in the Moon."

Although the film was not supposed to be anything but a fantasy, the spaceship Oberth designed for the picture was built very carefully, so that it solved many of the problems a spaceman would encounter in outer space. His spaceship, built over forty years ago, is similar to those designed today.

Hermann Oberth is the man responsible for Dr. Wernher von Braun's first interest in space flight. During the early days of the United States rocket program, he worked with Dr. von Braun at Redstone Arsenal in Huntsville, Alabama.

What is orbital flight? We know that all the planets are constantly moving — rotating on their own axis and, at the same time, revolving about the sun. If you wanted to go from earth to another planet, you would not be able to travel in a straight line. For example, suppose you aimed a rocket at Mars or Venus. By the time the rocket reached the spot at which you aimed it, the planet would have moved along in its orbit, and the rocket would miss its target entirely.

A simple way to explain the complexity of orbital flight is to watch two boys play a special kind of ball game. Usually, if two boys wanted to play catch, they would stand several feet apart and throw the ball back and forth. This would be the same as shooting a rocket from earth to another planet — if the two planets were standing still.

However, suppose we put one boy on a merry-go-round. He is moving in a circle, in the same way that the earth is rotating on its axis. If the boy on the merry-go-round waited until he was directly opposite the other boy on the ground before he threw the ball, the ball would never reach the other boy. As the ball was thrown from the moving merry-go-round, it would not only fly away from the merry-go-round, but it would also loop in the direction the merry-go-round was turning.

Suppose we place the boy on a mov-

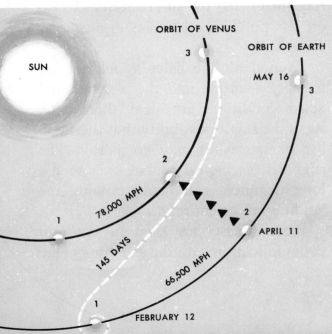

ORBIT OF VENUS

ORBIT OF EARTH

SUN

MAY 16

3

3

2

2

78,000 MPH

APRIL 11

1

145 DAYS

66,500 MPH

1

FEBRUARY 12

On February 12, 1961, the Russians fired a rocket which was to get to Venus, but its radio went dead shortly after blast-off, so it was impossible to determine whether or not a landing had been made. *Mariner IV*, the U. S. space probe, swooped past Mars on July 14, 1965 and transmitted photographs of the surface at a distance of 7,400 miles.

ing train instead of a merry-go-round. If he tried to throw the ball to the boy on the ground when his train was directly in front of the other boy, the ball would never reach its target. The ball would travel out away from the train, but it would also travel in the same direction as the train. It would travel in an arc. This train travel is similar to the earth's revolution in its orbit around the sun.

Actually, we would have to put the boy on a merry-go-round and then put the merry-go-round on a moving train if we wanted to duplicate the two motions of the earth — its rotation and its revolution in orbit.

It would take a lot of skill and practice for the two boys to play catch this way. Of course, in our solar system both planets are moving, and that would mean both boys would have to be on merry-go-rounds that are on moving trains. Imagine how difficult it would then be to play catch!

This is what is involved in orbital flight. Instead of firing a rocket in a straight line, we have to fire it in an arc and make adjustments and corrections for the rotations of both planets and the movements in their individual orbits.

At its nearest point, the earth and Venus are 26 million miles apart. If they were both perfectly still, we could fire a rocket or spaceship that would travel the 26 million miles and land on Venus. This, however, is a theoretical minimum distance.

The actual flight would be much longer, since in space we have the merry-go-round and train movements at very high speeds.

The Space-Age Guide to the Planets on page 48 shows the theoretical minimum flight times from the earth to the different planets. These are calculated on a straight-line flight if the planets were absolutely still and the spaceship were traveling at 25,000 miles an hour.

In reality, however, the flight would take much, much longer, since we would be traveling in an arc.

Orbital flight plans are made by special flight teams composed of astronomers, space technicians, mathematicians, astronauts and other specialists. Any flight to the moon or the planets depends upon the sun's gravitational pull. Despite the earth's sidereal and elliptical motions and the orbital pattern of the moon or a planet, the basic flight pattern recognizes that the sun continues to exert its "pull" on all bodies in our solar system.

How can we navigate in a spaceship?

Even if all the calculations are extremely accurate and the weather and space conditions are ideal, there is always the small possibility that the satellite or spaceship may go astray. The slightest veering off course, over such a long distance, can mean missing the landing target entirely.

Radio telescopes keep in constant communication with the satellite or ship

34

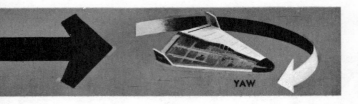

YAW

as it speeds through space. The information received from the many tracking stations is gathered in a control center. Here the information is interpreted with the assistance of a computer, so that fast, accurate answers are assured for all concerned.

To correct the course of a satellite or unmanned spaceship, radio signals are beamed at the ship in flight. These are picked up by the receiver and activate various controls. The firing of compressed air through special vents or the setting off of short rocket blasts will correct faults in flight. This was the method used by the Russians in the flight of their cosmonaut Major Gagarin. The space vehicle in which he traveled could be controlled only by the ground crew and not by the cosmonaut himself.

On the other hand, the United States'

Gemini and Apollo astronauts were able to maneuver their spacecraft by means of on-board instruments and computers. The astronauts maneuvered at will; some docked two craft end-to-end; some navigated to the moon, orbited it, and returned to earth.

Until the link-ups of *Soyuz 4* and *Soyuz 5* in early 1969, Russian cosmonauts could not maneuver their own spacecraft independently.

Only the slightest movement is necessary to alter the course of any rocket or spaceship. Instruments within the ship or on the ground receiving signals back from the ship, can tell if the vehicle is *yawing;* that is, if its nose is swinging from side to side.

Instruments can also tell if the vehicle is *pitching;* that is, if the nose is moving up or down. Once the air is fired through the special vents or a short rocket blast is used, the ship is back on course and on its way.

On May 6, 1961, American astronaut Alan Shepard made the first in-flight, controlled rocket trip into space. The rocket was launched at 9:34 A.M. and two minutes later, at 180,000 feet, the Mercury capsule separated from the rocket. At 9:37, Commander Shepard took over the control of this capsule, which was speeding through the air at 5,000 miles per hour. Six minutes later, he used retro-rockets to slow his speed as he started his descent toward earth. At 9:44, he released the parachute, and at 9:49, he landed in the water.

Shepard's instrument panel contained many indicator gauges and switches, a periscope through which to see and a lever to control the capsule's pitch, yaw and roll.

115 MILES

362

MILES

CAPE CANAVERAL

IMPACT

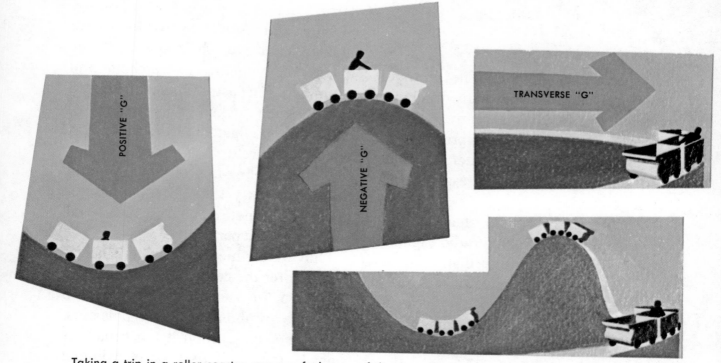

Taking a trip in a roller coaster, you can feel some of the sensations of a space flight. As the coaster comes rushing down, you are subjected to a positive "g" force. Your body feels as if it were being pushed through the seat, and the blood rushes out of your brain. At the top of a fast rise in the coaster, you are subjected to a negative "g" force. You feel as if you will continue going into the air, and extra blood is forced into your brain. When you go around a turn quickly, you are subjected to a transverse "g" force. Your body feels as if it will fly to one side; at this time, the blood in your body is being pushed in the same direction. You, like many pilots and spacemen, can stand this force better than the other "g's."

Why is re-entry a problem? Returning to the earth from space is as great a problem as leaving the earth for space. For many years scientists have worked to overcome the difficulties of re-entry. As you remember, we saw that there was no air in space. We start to encounter air in our atmosphere. The gases in our atmosphere are made of many little atoms. The closer to the earth, the greater the number of atoms in the air. This is true because air has weight, and the miles and miles of air on the top press down on the air below.

A spaceship traveling at thousands of miles an hour begins to come into the atmosphere. Here it comes into contact with the atoms in the air — it bumps into them, and the rubbing of the air atoms against the spaceship creates friction. Heat is created by this friction. As the spaceship comes closer to earth, the number of atoms in the air increases. This results in greater friction and, thus, in greater heat.

The surfaces of spaceships are covered with a special material, some of which burns and thus takes heat away from the inner walls. Some of the material chars, which provides a good heat insulator. Even with this heat-reducing material, the walls become hot.

Therefore, it is necessary to insulate the spaceship so that the man inside can withstand the heat.

Human Factors in Space Travel

Building a spaceship for space exploration is only part of the problem which we face in space exploration. Preparing the men to travel in these ships is the other part. Every advance in the science of transportation presents a problem and challenge to man.

What are the dangers to man in space travel?

For example, we know that when men go on long voyages into space, they will be exposed to cosmic radiation, extreme cold, and atmospheres where there is no available oxygen. They will be weightless for months, perhaps years. Most of these difficulties can be solved by proper construction of spaceships. But what about other problems created by extended space travel?

How will man's mind function in space travel?

It has been demonstrated that men can land on the moon, perform certain tasks, and return safely to earth. But what will happen during more extended visits to the moon — and on flights to other planets?

The *Skylab* program provided many of these answers. Three-man crews of astronauts spent 28, then 59, and later 84 days orbiting the earth in a space station. They were able to live and work in the new environment efficiently and without harmful effects.

Wearing a specially-made space suit, and lying down for the take-off as well as the landing, help the spaceman to withstand the high "g" pressures.

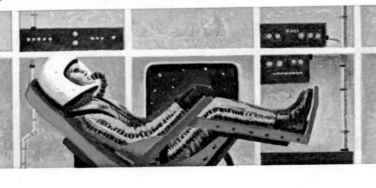

Interplanetary space encompasses a vast area, so that on any contemplated trip to another planet men will have to spend a great deal of time confined to their spaceships. A round trip to Mars, for example, could take about thirteen months.

With no precedent to guide them, space doctors and scientists must carefully evaluate the tolerances, the behavior, and the physical and mental health of lunar astronauts. Recent *Skylab* flights demonstrated that, except for a few minor problems, man's body adapts itself well to the new environment of space. So far, astronauts have been compatible and have been able to accomplish their oftentimes involved duties in situations requiring either quick mechanical response or cool judgment.

What is the g factor?

The normal pull of gravity on earth is a force that scientists call "one gravity" or 1 *g*. When a spaceship is taking off, it builds up speed very rapidly. At this time there is an increase in the *g* factor, just as there is when you are standing in an elevator and it starts to rise suddenly and rapidly. The earth is pulling on you just as it pulls on the spaceman.

Very high *g* forces can cause you to "black out" or lose consciousness, since the blood cannot circulate properly through your body. However, by wearing space clothing, or staying in a special position, spacemen can overcome the bad effects of this high *g* factor.

How does a space suit help a pilot?

The space suit provides an essential safety factor for the spaceman just as it does for high-altitude pilots. It helps to control temperature and air pressure and assures its wearer of a supply of oxygen. The suit is made of a strong, lightweight material that fits the body like a glove. Like the glove on your hand, there is a minute space between the suit and the body in which there is air.

Pressure control is one of the more important reasons for using a space suit. As we go higher above the earth, the air pressure decreases. The normal human being has about five quarts of blood in his body. If you went up to

A controlled dive of a conventional airplane can put a man into a weightless state for about a minute.

25,000 feet — about 4¾ miles — above the earth without a space suit or without a pressure cabin in a plane, the oxygen in your blood would bubble out as a gas. The normal five quarts of blood would need the same space as fifteen quarts on the ground. At 50,000 feet, the oxygen gas would expand further, making the space needed for the five quarts almost the same as eighty-five quarts on the ground. You can readily see that your body would virtually explode as the blood expanded.

In addition, the space suit is connected to several tanks in the spaceship. One tank maintains the proper air pressure; another supplies the oxygen; still another takes the harmful carbon dioxide, which you exhale, out of the suit. Furthermore, the oxygen supplied in the suit is temperature-controlled so that no matter how cold it gets outside the spaceship — or inside — your body remains comfortable. Space suits were not needed inside the *Skylab,* but the astronauts wore them when they worked outside the orbiting space station.

To help overcome the high *g* forces to which the spaceman is exposed during take-off, he also uses a special seat. This seat is something like a bed, so that his body appears to be lying down in the ship. In this position it is easier for his heart to pump the blood to all the parts of his body as compared with a standing or sitting position.

How does a spaceman train for the high g factors?

To prepare the space traveler for the high *g* factors he will experience in take-off and in landing, he is trained in a *centrifuge* (CEN-tri-fuge). This is a large machine with a rotating arm to which a model cabin of a spaceship is attached. The motor of the machine rotates the arm at faster and faster speeds, and the spaceman in the cabin is thus subjected to increased *g* pressure. Some of the astronauts have been subjected to a force as high as 40 *g*. If the man normally weighed 200 pounds, his body would weigh four tons or 8,000 pounds under this force. Many spacemen have been able to take this pressure for short intervals and still remain conscious.

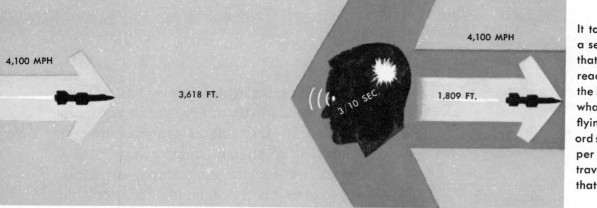

4,100 MPH

3,618 FT.

3/10 SEC.

4,100 MPH

1,809 FT.

It takes about 3/10 of a second for the image that the eye sees to reach the brain and for the brain to tell the pilot what to do. If you were flying at the X-15's record speed of 4,100 miles per hour, you would be traveling 1,809 feet in that 3/10 of a second.

How does "weightlessness" affect man?

Have you ever taken a ride on a roller coaster? Have you ever been in an elevator when it started to descend suddenly and quickly? If you have, you've experienced "weightlessness." The sensation we feel when the parts of the body press downward against each other for support is the feeling of weight. Once this pressure is removed, we feel weightless. In technical language, this is known as a *zero g force.*

For some people it is an uncomfortable feeling. They are so upset that they cannot think of anything else; nor can they react properly when they are required to pull a lever or read an instrument dial. All they want is to "land," or to feel normal again. For others, weightlessness appears to be no problem. They glide through "space" feeling as if they were swimming underwater. They can move and react normally.

Astronauts in space are weightless. A rookie astronaut is taken for a ride in a transport plane that dives and pulls up at a calculated angle, whereupon he floats about weightlessly for about a minute (see illustration on pages 38 and 39). All astronauts have lived and worked normally during space flights.

Astronauts have become accustomed to weightlessness for as long as three months. Doctors now believe that man can adapt to space flights to the planets.

How important is "reaction time" in space travel?

Flying at high speeds in a spaceship could create problems for the spaceman. One of these is the time he takes to react to signals from the ground or warnings from his instrument panel. Studies of people's reactions by scientists disclosed that it takes about three-tenths of a second to react. For example, if you put your hand in some very hot water, it would take about three-tenths of a second before you pulled it out. That is the time it takes for the signal from nerves in your hand to reach your brain — for your brain to decide what to do — and for your brain to order your muscles to pull your hand away. This interval is called *normal reaction time.*

When preparing for the manned space program, U. S. scientists wanted to test reaction time during weightlessness and increased g force. They taught several chimpanzees to pull different levers, depending on a signal which flashed on a screen. When the chimps pulled the correct lever, they were rewarded with a banana-flavored pellet,

If the chimpanzee pushed the right lever, it was rewarded with a banana-flavored pellet.

but when they made a mistake, they received nothing. The chimps learned quickly. One of them became so adept, he was able to pull the right lever a hundred times in a minute — more than one each second.

Then, in February, 1961, one of the astrochimps, named Ham, was lobbed into space for a short suborbital flight. Ham, weightless and experiencing increased g force, activated the levers without any change in the reaction time he had scored on earth.

What scientists learned from Ham has been borne out by all astronauts: weightlessness and moderately increased g force do not cause a significant slowing of reaction time.

Maneuvering a craft in the vastness of space today is somewhat like driving an automobile on a lonely road—small errors of speed and direction can be corrected safely without split-second reaction time. But someday, space near the earth might become crowded with spacecraft. Split-second reaction time will then be a matter of life and death. The situation will be more like driving an automobile in heavy fast-moving traffic. *Apollo 8* started for the moon at a speed of more than 25,000 miles per hour and reentered the earth's atmosphere at almost the same speed. At such a fast rate a spaceship moves more than two miles before an astronaut can even react to a needed change in speed or direction. For this reason, departing and landing spacecraft will probably be maneuvered automatically by flight controllers aboard orbiting "control towers."

Steps to the Moon

Eleven years after *Sputnik 1* opened the Space Age, three American astronauts aboard the spacecraft

What were the preparations for the moon voyage?

Apollo 8 orbited the moon.

The moon-orbiting journey of *Apollo 8* went so smoothly that it is easy to forget the vast amount of preparation that made it possible.

First, there were the unmanned satellites gathering information about space near the earth. The United States' first satellite, *Explorer 1*, orbiting the earth

In February, 1961, an astro-chimp named Ham became the first earthly creature to operate controls in a space capsule.

in February, 1958, confirmed a belt of radiation surrounding the earth which could be harmful to astronauts passing through it. Special radiation shields had to be built into spacecraft.

Dozens of satellites in the intervening years counted meteroids hurtling along in space near the earth. The radioed reports of these obstacles enabled scientists to decide if they would be too much of a hazard.

On the ground, engineers developed more and more powerful rockets until they had, in *Saturn 5,* one strong enough to boost a moonship into space.

Telescopes alone are not powerful enough to enable scientists on earth to explore the moon's surface closely, and so, to choose a future landing site, cameras, instruments, and analytical devices were first sent to the moon.

How were moon sites chosen?

Project Ranger, the initial program, consisted of sending television cameras to the moon by lunar spacecraft. Each camera was designed to start taking pictures at a distance of a few hundred miles from the moon's surface and to continue in operation until the lunar spacecraft crashed. The first six *Rangers* failed in their missions — they either went into orbit around the earth, missed the moon, or crashed into the moon without sending back any pictures. *Rangers 7, 8,* and *9,* however, carried out their missions perfectly, sending back to earth a total of more than 17,000 pictures. The closest picture was taken only three-quarters of a mile above the moon's surface, showing objects as small as ten inches.

Next came *Project Surveyor.* Using information and technical knowledge gained by means of the *Ranger* project, cameras and other equipment were soft-landed on the moon. The cameras were only a foot or two above the lunar surface and sent back to earth thousands of close-up photographs that showed in detail the kind of surface a manned spacecraft would have to land on. One *Surveyor* not only had a camera, but a claw, as well, which dug a small trench in the moon's dustlike "soil" while the camera photographed it. From the amount of power expended by the claw in digging, scientists were able to calculate approximately the firmness of the moon's crust.

Following *Project Surveyor,* the U. S. sent up *Lunar Orbiters,* spacecraft which went into orbit around the moon and whose cameras scanned almost the whole lunar surface, transmitting pictures back to earth. Scientists used photo maps, together with information accumulated by *Ranger* and *Surveyor* spacecraft, to decide on an appropriate landing site.

Finally, on Christmas Eve, 1968, three astronauts aboard the *Apollo 8* spacecraft had a close look at the moon while orbiting less than 70 miles above its surface. One thing these astronauts proved was that, although instruments can reveal much information about space and astronomical bodies, the instruments still need considerable development before they can do as well as a man in the same place.

For centuries man tried to guess or **What is the topography of the moon?** learn what the surface of the moon was like. But even the most powerful telescopes could provide information about only one side of the moon, since its rotation (on its axis) and its revolution about the earth are synchronized so that there is just one side facing the earth at all times.

The surface of the moon as ascertained to date has four distinct characteristics. First, there are the lofty mountains. The Leibnitz and Dorfel Mountains in the moon's southern hemisphere exceed an estimated height of thirty thousand feet. Second, there are the broad dark plains or "seas" of the moon, visible with the naked eye on a clear night. (It is on just one of these seas, the Sea of Tranquility, that the footprints of man's first visit to our neighbor in space still remain.) Craters are the third and most outstanding feature of the moon. They are very deep and very wide, and can be found almost everywhere on the surface. A crater known as Clavius, for example, is 16,-000 feet deep and 145 miles in diameter. Finally, there are the rilles — long deep crevices that are sometimes a mile or more wide at the top.

The "dark" side of the moon, the side which is never seen from earth, was first photographed in 1959 by *Luna 2,* a Soviet satellite. In 1967 and 1968, orbiting spacecraft sent to the moon by the United States took thousands of detailed pictures of both sides of the moon. From this evidence, and from subsequent manned missions, we learned that the hidden side of the moon looks much like the side we have always seen, having mountains, "seas," craters, and rocks.

During the *Apollo 9* flight the lunar **What did Apollo 9 achieve?** module (LM) was separated from the command ship and flown more than a hundred miles away. Colonel James A. McDivitt and Colonel David R. Scott were then able to steer the lunar lander back to the command ship for the relinking, or docking maneuver.

In another key maneuver, Russell L. Schweickart, pilot of the command ship, opened the LM hatch and stepped out onto a platform to test the spacesuit and oxygen-supplying backpack that men would use when they landed on the moon.

Combining the features of its two immediate predecessors, **What was Apollo 10's mission?** *Apollo 10* managed to go a little further in all departments. The lunar module came within 9.4 miles of the moon's surface and circled the moon's equator. This time the lunar module and the command ship engineered a link-up about sixty-nine miles from the moon. And this time there were color television pictures, photographs of the intended lunar landing site on the Sea of Tranquility, and extensive tests of the effect the moon's weak gravitational pull might have on the accuracy of the flight.

Exploring the moon.

Less than twelve minutes after *Apollo 11* was launched from Cape Kennedy, the craft shot into earth orbit. It was the morning of July 17, 1969. Another firing of the third-stage engine eventually propelled *Apollo 11* out of earth orbit and on toward the moon at a speed of 24,200 miles an hour.

How did Apollo 11 start out?

Neil A. Armstrong and his fellow astronauts, Lieutenant Colonel Michael Collins and Colonel Edwin E. ("Buzz") Aldrin, Jr., then separated their spacecraft from the *Saturn* rocket's third stage by the automatic firing of explosive bolts. The command ship pivoted and locked its nose into the lunar landing craft, still housed at the top of the *Saturn* rocket. Finally, after *Apollo 11* had traveled more than fifty thousand miles, the command ship *Columbia* and the lunar module *Eagle* pulled free of the rocket stage.

Astronauts in lunar module prepare to return to orbiting command module.

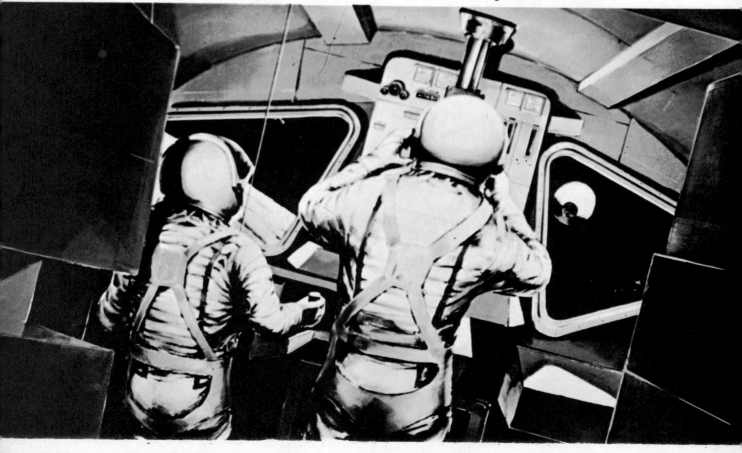

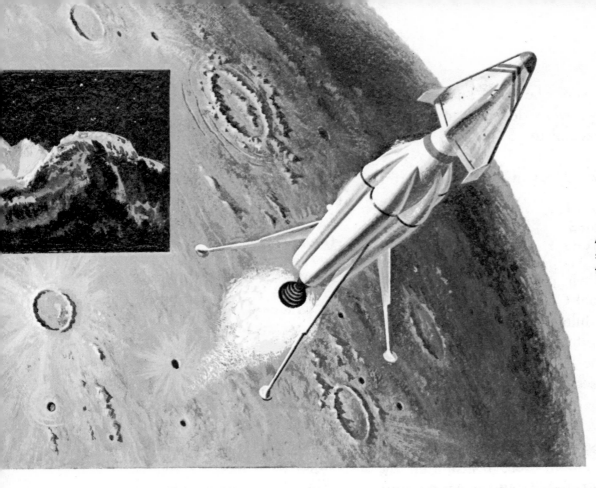

Artist's conception of a space vehicle's blast-off from the lunar surface.

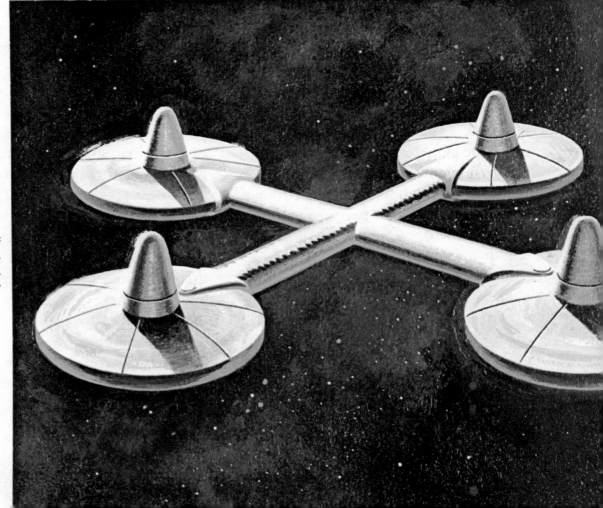

Artist's conception of an orbiting space station, dubbed the "Mexican Hat Space Station."

These were the men and the machines that were destined to become part of space history.

As *Apollo 11* began its eleventh orbit

What was the "giant leap for mankind"?

of the moon, astronauts Neil Armstrong and Edwin ("Buzz") Aldrin, wearing their pressurized space suits, left Michael Collins alone in the command module and crawled through a connecting tunnel to the lunar module. Then came the undocking. LM *Eagle* was released and began its descent to the surface of the moon.

At 4:17 P.M. (E.D.S.T.), on July 20, 1969, these words, the first ever issued from the moon, were transmitted by Neil Armstrong: "Houston, Tranquility Base here. The *Eagle* has landed."

Six and a half hours later, as millions of people on earth shared the adventure by means of television and radio, Neil Armstrong gingerly placed his left foot on the brownish lunar surface and announced, "That's one small step for a man, one giant leap for mankind." And nineteen minutes later Edwin ("Buzz") Aldrin became the second man to set foot on the moon. The two men scooped up soil and rock samples for analysis, set up a miniature seismic station for detecting possible tremors or moon-quakes, and positioned a reflector that would bounce laser beams back to earth. They also put up — and later took down — a banner of aluminum foil facing the sun that would detect the nuclei of such gases as neon, argon and krypton.

Subsequent *Apollo* flights were made to explore other parts of the lunar surface. During later trips, astronauts traveled about on the moon in a *Lunar Rover* vehicle, which looks like a dune buggy. This vehicle enabled the explorers to travel farther than previous *Apollo* astronauts.

Scientists believe it would be feasible to

Can man live on the moon?

establish a base on the moon so that man could stay there for extended periods of time. Such a possibility, of course, is not without its additional risks. A man on the moon (and his equipment) would be exposed to extreme temperature changes — it ranges from 250° F. during its day to −280° F. at night. There is only the slightest trace of an atmosphere on the moon, since a weak gravity is unable to keep it intact, and so, with a lack of such gas mass there can be no weather as we know it — no snow or rain, no clouds, no wind. This lack of atmosphere, or even the very thin atmosphere, on the moon creates another problem. Micrometeorites (very small meteorites) constantly pass through space above the moon without meeting any resistance. On earth, micrometeorites (or even meteorites) burn up because of the friction that is created when they pass through our atmosphere. On the moon, though, these small particles strike the surface without hindrance. Some of the larger micrometeorites, traveling at high speed, may puncture the skin of a spaceship, the roof of a spaceport, or a man's space suit.

Considerably less fuel is needed for a space vehicle to return to earth than is required for a trip from the earth to the moon.

Why is a trip back to earth easier?

With the moon's gravitational pull being much less than the earth's, less force is needed to propel a craft away from its mass. The weaker gravity means that a craft will travel for a shorter time before being influenced by the earth's gravity. At this point it can begin its "fall" to earth because it is being attracted, or pulled, to the home planet. Speed increases as the ship approaches earth, and retro-rockets are used to decrease this speed as the ship enters the atmosphere, preparatory to landing.

Exploring the Planets!

Not long after man has built bases on the moon, he will turn to explore the nearby planets.

How will man travel to Mars?

Venus is the nearest planet, but it will probably not be the first one that man tries to visit. The space probes sent to Venus by the United States and Russia have revealed an inhospitable planet with such harsh surface conditions that manned exploration would be just about impossible. On the other hand, our next nearest neighbor, Mars, is a planet upon which a manned exploration would not be too difficult, especially after man has learned to explore the moon.

The temperature of Mars during the day is warm enough for a man to wear only light clothing. At night, the temperature is extremely low, but man has learned to cope with even colder temperatures on the moon. Mars' thin atmosphere has some water vapor in it, which could be condensed to usable water. There does not seem to be any oxygen in the Martian atmosphere, but man's experience in space has taught him to explore by carrying his own oxygen supply.

Mars is 144 times as far from the earth as the moon. A huge spaceship will be needed to carry all the equipment and supplies necessary to keep the astronauts alive on their way to and from this planet, all of the instruments needed for exploring, and sufficient fuel to maneuver the spacecraft and bring it back. Boosting such a spaceship off the earth would require a Saturn-type booster many times larger than the *Sat-*

urn 5, perhaps one tall as the Empire State Building!

One solution would be to place in orbit the necessary parts of the spaceship and assemble them in space. Once the Mars spaceship was fully built in space, supplies and fuel could be ferried to it, and finally, the exploration team of astronauts would board it. From orbit, they would be able to blast off for Mars using only a fraction of the power needed to lift off the earth.

Space-Age Guide to the Planets

Planet	Mercury	Venus	Earth	Mars	Jupiter	Saturn	Uranus	Neptune	Pluto
Distance from the Sun (millions of miles)	36.0	67.2	92.9	141.5	483.9	886.0	1783.0	2791.7	3670.0
Theoretical Minimum Time to Reach Planet from Earth	83 days	45 days		58 days	1 year, 8 months	3 years, 5 months	7 years, 5 months	12 years, 2 months	12 years, 2 months
Diameter (miles)	3,100	7,700	7,927	4,200	85,750	71,150	32,000	27,600	3,700
Time to Complete One Orbital Revolution Around the Sun (measured in Earth time)	88 days	225 days	365.26 days	687 days	11 years, 314 days	29 years, 168 days	84 years, 7 days.	164 years, 285 days	248 years, 146 days
Length of Day (measured in Earth time)	88 days	225 days	23 hours, 56 minutes	24 hours, 37 minutes	9 hours, 55 minutes	10 hours, 14 minutes	10 hours, 49 minutes	15 hours, 40 minutes	16 hours
Surface Gravity (measured in terms of 1 g on Earth)	0.35	0.88	1.00	0.38	2.64	1.17	0.96	1.5	0.16
Weight of a Man on the Planet if He Weighed 200 Pounds on Earth	70	176	200	76	528	234	184	280	32
Escape Velocity (miles per hour)	9,700	23,000	25,000	11,500	133,200	79,200	49,320	57,600	22,000
Temperature on Surface	−260°F. to 650°F.	800°F.	−90°F. to 136°F.	−200°F. to 85°F.	−215°F. average	−285°F. average	−360°F. average	−375°F. average	−300°F. (est.)
Number of Moons	0	0	1	2	13	10	5	2	0

THE HOW AND WHY WONDER BOOK OF

STARS

By Norman Hoss
Illustrated by James Ponter

Edited under the supervision of
Dr. Paul E. Blackwood
Washington, D. C.

Text and illustrations approved by

Oakes A. White
Brooklyn Children's Museum
Brooklyn, New York

GROSSET & DUNLAP · Publishers · NEW YORK

INTRODUCTION

This book about stars is one in a series of *How and Why Wonder Books* planned to open doors of scientific knowledge to young readers. It has been prepared to help young people explore, in a systematic way, the wonders of the universe. It will help them discover what astronomers — both ancient and modern — have learned and stimulate children to raise new and unanswered questions. This is in the true spirit of science.

Exploring the stars has always been fascinating to people everywhere. Perhaps this is because our neighbors in the sky are so much a part of everyone's experience. Everyone can look up and behold the heavens. Yet "just looking" does not tell us all we want to know about the untold thousands of galaxies and the unimaginable vastness of space. Thus we are left with a sense of wonder and awe. It has always been so.

But if "just looking" at the stars does not give us all the answers to our questions, then we must turn to the vast store of knowledge gathered by the astronomers. They have used special instruments and mathematics as well as their experienced eyes to get answers, and much of what they have learned is contained in the following pages.

This book will enable young people to observe the heavens with increased respect for what is known, and greater appreciation for what is yet unknown.

Paul E. Blackwood

Dr. Blackwood is a professional employee in the U. S. Office of Education. This book was edited by him in his private capacity and no official support or endorsement by the Office of Education is intended or should be inferred.

Library of Congress Catalog Card Number: 61-1545
ISBN: 0-448-05064-1 (WONDER EDITION)
ISBN: 0-448-04005-0 (TRADE EDITION)
ISBN: 0-448-03841-2 (LIBRARY EDITION)
1983 PRINTING

Contents

LIGHTS IN THE SKY

If you look up at the sky on a clear night, what do you see? There are thousands of lights against a dark background. Let's pretend at first that we know nothing but what we can see. Then it will be easy to understand what people first thought about these lights in the sky and how they slowly pieced together the wonderful facts and ideas that make up the science of astronomy.

What can we see in the sky?

Let's say that we are standing in a place where there are no buildings or trees or mountains to block our view of the sky, for instance on the deck of a ship in the ocean. The sky will look to us the same as it looked to the earliest man on earth. In thousands of years there have been no changes that you could tell by just looking.

Beyond our ship all we can see is water and sky. It is as if we were alone in an empty house. The shape of the house looks very simple. The surface of the ocean makes the floor. It appears to be flat and perfectly round. We seem to be exactly in the center of it. The house appears to be covered by a dome. It is as if the sky were a half of a hollow

ball, a great bowl turned upside down on a flat disk which is the earth. Looking all around us we can see where the sky and earth seem to meet in a circle. We name this circle the horizon.

As we look up from the horizon in any direction, there are the lights of the stars in the dome of the sky. On some nights the moon appears and the fainter stars fade from view. On dark nights a band of milky light extends across part of the sky. By day the blinding light of the sun is all we can see in the sky.

This is the way the universe looked to

What did primitive people believe about the sky?

primitive people, and so it is the way they believed it to be. They believed the earth was flat, because it looks flat. They believed the horizon was the edge of the earth, because you can't see anything beyond it. And they believed that the sky was the dome-shaped roof of the world.

Some thought that the stars were lights attached to the sky, just as we have electric lights in the ceiling of a room. Others believed there was a bright heaven beyond the sky and that the stars were holes in the dome letting in light from heaven.

This was man's first idea of the universe (a word that includes everything that exists). We now know these early beliefs are not true, but they were based on what could be seen. If there were no one to tell us what men have learned, we would start with this same view of the universe.

Ancient people were not satisfied

What do myths tell of the sky?

with this description of the "how" of the stars. They wanted to explain the "why." In trying to do this they made up stories called myths about gods and heroes. There were many myths about the sky among people in different places at different times. Myths tried to explain such things as why the sun rises and sets and why the moon appears to change shape from night to night.

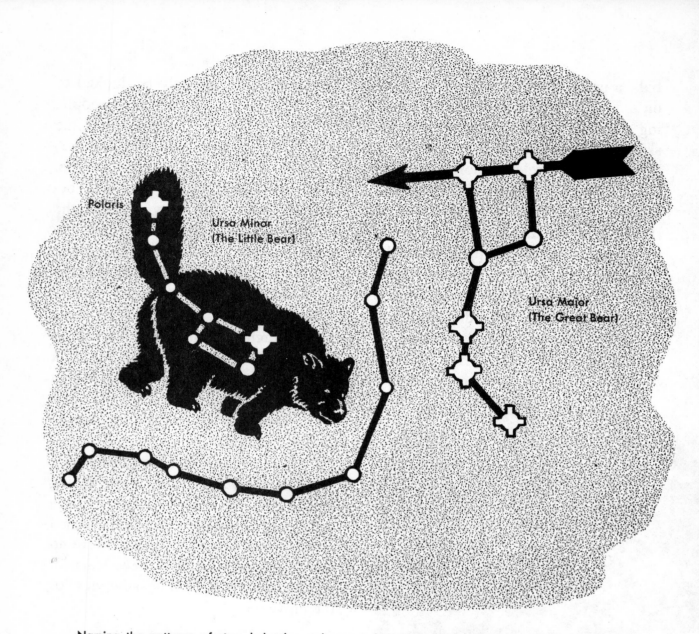

Naming the patterns of stars helped people remember them and use them to find their way at night. Notice how the "pointer stars" in Ursa Major help you find the North Star, Polaris.

Polaris

Ursa Minor
(The Little Bear)

Ursa Major
(The Great Bear)

We are not interested in the explanations that myths give for what happens in the sky. We read myths nowadays because some of them are beautiful stories that tell deep truths about human nature. In this book we are interested in myths for only one reason. They provided a map of the sky, which, with some changes, astronomers still use today.

When you look at the stars the first thing you notice is that some are brighter than others. Then you notice that some of the bright ones make patterns that are easy to remember. These patterns of stars are called constellations. The ancient Greeks gave them names and made up myths about them. By naming the con-

What are constellations?

stellations, they created a map of the sky. Just as a map of the United States shows that Chicago is in Illinois, the map of the constellations shows that Polaris, the North Star, is in the constellation Ursa Minor, the Little Bear. Don't expect to recognize the constellations from the creatures they are named for. The star maps in the back of the book show the constellations.

As soon as men recognized a pattern of stars as a constellation, they were able to make a great discovery. The stars move. A single constellation can be found in different parts of the sky at different times. But the patterns themselves never change; all the stars seem to move together. It seemed obvious to ancient men that the sky itself moved and all the stars were attached to it. But were they all? As men watched the sky they discovered that a few of the brightest stars did not stay in a particular constellation. At different times of the year they could be seen in different constellations. These lights were called wanderers. From the Greek word for "wanderer" we get our word *planet*.

There were five planets that the Greeks

How were the planets named? could see, and they named them after gods (we now use their Roman names): Jupiter, the ruler of the gods; Venus, the goddess of love; Mars, the god of war; Mercury, the messenger of the gods; and Saturn, Father Time.

The ancient watchers of the sky also saw that sometimes there were lights that blazed across the sky and disappeared. These were thought to be stars that had fallen from the sky.

There was one other thing that an-cient people sometimes saw in the sky, a bright light with a long shining tail. These comets, as they are called, appeared many years apart. Ordinarily no one sees more than one in his lifetime. Up until recent times many people were terrified when a comet appeared. Sometimes they thought the end of the world had come.

Everything, then—except man-made satellites—that we can see in the sky today with our eyes alone was known to ancient men: sun, moon, stars, the Milky Way, planets, meteors (which is the name we now give to the "falling stars"), and comets.

When comets such as this appeared in the sky, ancient people were frightened.

EARTH AND SKY

By the sixth century B.C., in Greece,

When did men first guess the earth was round? there were men calling them-selves philoso-phers who tried to explain the facts of nature without using the stories of mythology.

From the fact that sun, moon and stars set in the west and then rise in the east the next day, these men rea-soned that everything in the sky must go around the earth every day. They also noted that some stars to the north never set, but move in circles around

As a boat moves away, its sail seems to "sink" below the horizon. This shows that the earth is curved.

the North Star, Polaris. It seemed clear to them that the sky was not a bowl, a half of a ball, as it appeared to primitive men. They pictured it as a whole ball, a hollow sphere.

In science, one idea leads to another, and the idea of the celestial sphere, as the ball of the sky was called, led to a more important discovery. If the sky is a sphere, philosophers reasoned, it would seem proper that the earth is also shaped like a ball. This idea was taught by a few philosophers as early as the fifth century B.C. This was two thousand years before Ferdinand Magellan's

ships proved the earth was round by sailing around it.

Learned men called attention to familiar facts that showed the earth was curved. When a ship disappears over the horizon, they pointed out, its mast remains visible for a time after the hull has gone out of sight, just as if the ship were going over a hill.

More than two centuries before Christ, a Greek named Eratosthenes, librarian of the great museum in Alexandria, Egypt, actually figured the distance around the earth with near-perfect accuracy.

With the work of the great astronomer

How did ancient astronomers picture the universe?

Ptolemy, who lived in Alexandria in the second century A.D., the ancient view of the universe was completed. It is shown in the model. At the center is the globe of the earth. Around it is the bigger globe of the celestial sphere. Its axis (the line on which it turns) runs through the center of the earth. The stars are fixed to the sphere, so that as it rotates from east to west, the stars turn with it, going once around the earth every twenty-four hours.

This view of the universe explained the motions of the stars satisfactorily, even though it was not correct. This often happens in science. But one thing Ptolemy was unable to explain was the motions of the planets. He made up a remarkably clever — and complicated — picture of how the planets move, but it did not quite fit the facts. Ptolemy was wrong on two vital counts. He thought the earth was the center of the universe

Although we can't feel it, the earth is hurtling through space.

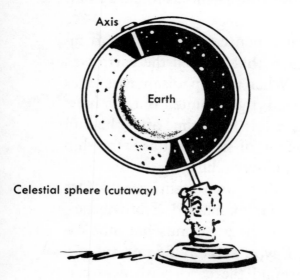

Celestial sphere (cutaway)

Axis

Earth

A model of the ancient idea of the universe

and he thought that the earth stood still while everything else moved around it.

Curiously enough one man had the right answers on these two points some 500 years before Ptolemy. A philosopher named Aristarchus suggested that the apparent movement of the stars is caused by the earth turning on its axis. And he even suggested that the earth moves around the sun. It is not surprising that his ideas were ignored. It is hard to believe that we are riding on a spinning space ship zipping around the sun.

ASTRONOMY AND ASTROLOGY

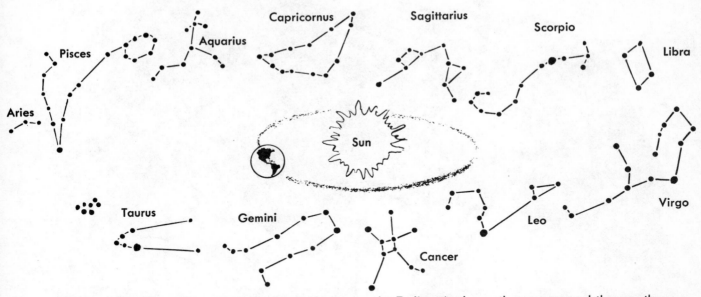

Twelve constellations form a circle in the sky known as the Zodiac. As the earth moves around the sun, the sun appears to rise and set in a part of the sky marked by one after another of these constellations.

SO THE ancient view of the universe remained unchanged and unquestioned for some 1,500 years. You might think that people simply lost interest in the stars, but this was not true. Some men throughout the Middle Ages watched the sky with deep interest. They did not make discoveries as the Greeks had, because they were not interested in astronomy. They were interested in astrology.

What is astrology? Astrology was an ancient system of magic. Astrologers thought they could tell what was going to happen by studying the positions of the sun, moon, and planets. Astrology was based on the fact that the courses of these bodies are confined to a narrow band of the sky. This band was named the Zodiac and was divided into twelve parts called signs. The signs were named for the constellations in those twelve regions of the sky. Because of a "wobble" in the earth's motion the constellations are no longer seen in the signs bearing their names. But there are still people who believe in astrology.

Unless you carefully study the sky and apply mathematics to what you see, it is just as easy to believe the ideas of astrology as the facts of astronomy. Before people came to trust the methods of science, they saw no reason to accept what astronomers told them. Astronomy deals with facts that are not apparent in everyday life. You can't bring a star into a laboratory — you can only study its light.

THE SOLAR SYSTEM

Nicolaus Copernicus

WE SHOULD NOT be surprised that the first attempt to change the ancient view of the universe met with strong opposition. Nicolaus Copernicus, a Polish monk, was the first to disagree publicly with the accepted scheme. His book was not published until a few days before his death in 1543, so the task of defending his ideas fell to others.

How did Copernicus change men's view of the universe?

After studying the planets for years, Copernicus concluded that their motions could be explained only one way. He decided that the earth itself is one of the planets and that they all move around the sun. He was unable to prove his plan, because observations of the sky were so inaccurate at the time. But he did work out the correct order of the planets in distance from the sun.

It was the great Italian scientist Galileo who bore the brunt of defending the Copernican system. With the aid of the newly invented telescope, he was able to add additional evidence for the new system and he wrote eloquently in defense of it. He was finally imprisoned for teaching it. Old and ill, he was forced to deny that the earth moved around the sun. But his work had already been done. Copernicus' view of the universe had been taken up by more and more of the growing number of scientists.

It was the patient observations of the Danish astronomer Tycho Brahe that made it possible finally to work out an accurate picture of the solar system, as the sun and its planets are called. From Brahe's long series of precise observations, Johann Kepler in 1609 figured out that the paths of the planets around the sun were not circles, as Copernicus had assumed. Kepler found the orbits are slightly flattened circles — a figure that is known as an ellipse. The illustration and caption show a simple way to draw an ellipse. The sun is located in this figure at one of the two points known as focuses which are indicated in the illustration by the tacks.

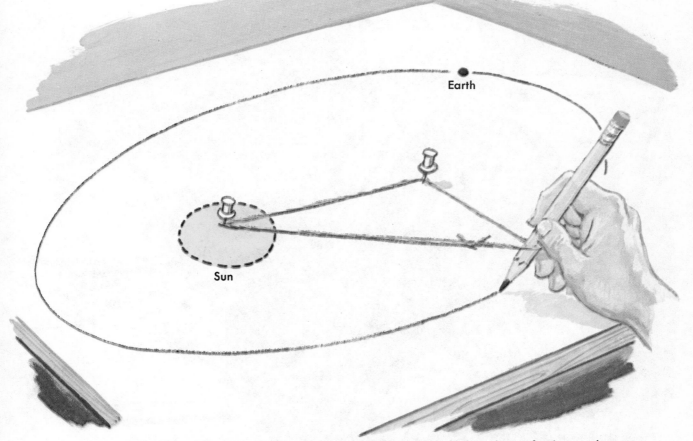

To draw an ellipse, place two tacks a convenient distance apart. Make a loop of string as shown. The larger the loop is, the bigger the ellipse. Put a pencil through the loop and draw the string snug. If you keep the loop tight, the pencil can move in only one path. This path is an ellipse. The closer the tacks are together, the more like a circle the ellipse will look.

It then remained for Isaac Newton to explain why the planets move in this pattern and what keeps the whole solar system in its pattern. He stated that every piece of matter attracts every other piece. This force he called gravity. He did not try to say what gravity is, but he showed by mathematics exactly how it works. The pull of gravity between two objects is greater the "heavier" they are — that is, the more "mass" they have. The attraction increases the closer together objects are.

What holds the solar system together?

It would be interesting to continue to follow the story, step by step, of how men have pieced together their knowledge of the skies, but this would require a huge book. Since the time of Newton, more and more scientists have made more and more discoveries. The rest of this book tells about the universe as scientists now know it. Once we have seen that the earth is not the center of the universe, we no longer have to study the heavenly bodies only as they appear from the earth. We can imagine that we are looking at them from any spot in space that gives us the best view.

Sir Isaac Newton

THE SUN

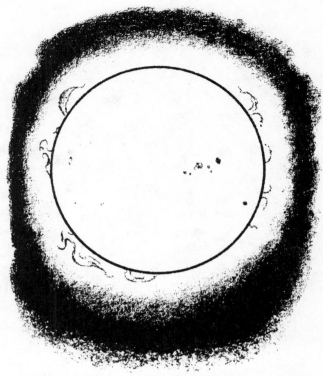

The sunspots shown are huge storms covering areas larger than the earth's diameter. The flares around the edge are great eruptions of fiery gases thousands of miles long.

WE SHALL naturally look first at the sun, then at the sun's family of planets, of which our earth is a member. The family is called the solar system, from the Latin word *solus,* for sun.

Throughout all the centuries, up until man first released atomic energy in the 1940's, the sun has been earth's only power plant. All the usable energy on earth has come from the sun. When primitive man burned a log of wood, he was releasing energy from the sun's rays stored in the wood by the processes of life in the tree. The energy from the food we eat can be traced to the sun in the same way. Electricity produced by water falling over a dam is energy from the sun because the sun's heat had to raise up the water by evaporation before it could fall back to the earth as rain and run down the rivers.

Why doesn't the sun burn up? For centuries men wondered how the sun could continue to put out so much heat energy without burning up. The answer we now know is that the sun does not burn. It is an atomic-energy furnace that produces its energy by the same process as the hydrogen bomb. The immediate question that arises is: "Why doesn't the sun blow up like a hydrogen bomb?" And the answer is: because it is so big. Remember, Newton discovered that every particle of matter attracts every other particle. In the sun there are so many atoms that their attraction for each other is strong enough to resist the fantastic forces — greater than those in the hydrogen bomb—that are thrusting atoms apart.

15

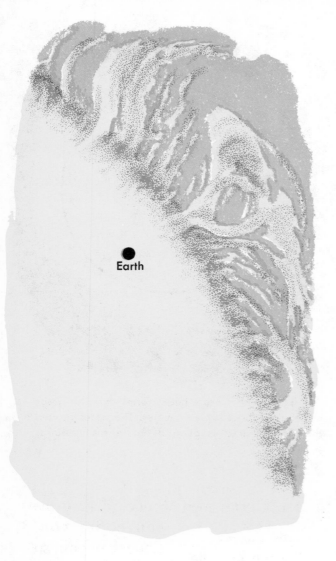

Earth

What is the sun made of? Even though it is very large compared to the earth, the sun is really only an "average" star. There are stars hundreds of times the size of the sun.

The sun is all gas. It may be hard to imagine a ball of gas in space. We think of gas as a substance that escapes unless we keep it closed in, like the gas in a toy balloon. But again, it is gravity that holds the gas together in the sun, just as the gravity of the earth holds its layer of air around it. The gravity of the sun is vastly greater than that of the earth. The attraction of the sun's atoms toward its center compresses them so much that a piece from the middle of the sun would be heavier than a block of iron the same size. Yet the center of the sun has not been squeezed into a solid core or even into liquid. It is so hot in the sun that nothing can exist as a solid or liquid.

How big is the sun? The sun is more than a million times the size of the earth. Its diameter is 864,000 miles as compared with the earth's 7,927 miles. But the sun is not nearly a million times heavier than the earth. Its mass is only about 332,000 times as great as the earth's. (The word "only" sounds funny with a figure that, in terms of weight on the surface of the earth, would mean 4,380,000,000,-000,000,000,000,000,000 pounds.) The sun must be made of lighter stuff than the earth. If the earth were as big as the sun, it would weigh four times as much.

How hot is the sun? The heat at the center of the sun is estimated at about 35,000,000 degrees on the same kind of Fahrenheit scale that the weatherman uses. Outward from the center the temperature grows gradually lower. At the "surface," the face of the sun from which we get our heat, it is only 11,000 degrees. (There's that word "only" again. About the hottest thing we can think of on earth is the inside of a steel-making furnace. The sun's face is many times hotter.)

THE PLANETS

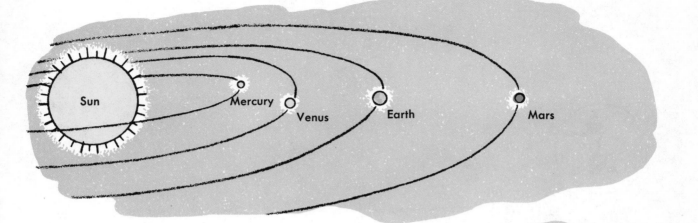

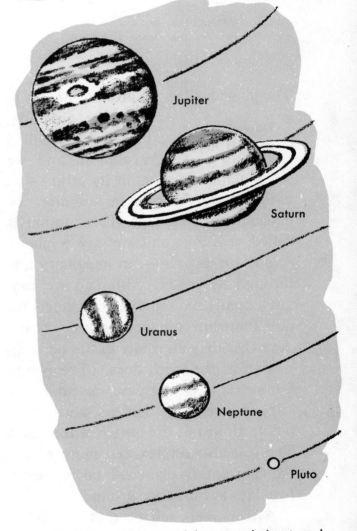

If we could stand in outer space we could see tiny specks of light around the great blazing ball of the sun. These are the planets. They do not give off light of their own. We can see them only by sunlight reflected from them.

How do the planets shine?

We now know of nine planets; one of these is our earth. Of the other eight, four are very like the earth — globes of rock of comparable size. The other four are giants compared with the earth and they are made of much lighter stuff. Mercury, Venus, Mars and Pluto are called terrestrial planets (from the Latin word for earth), because they are like the earth. The giant planets are Jupiter, Saturn, Uranus and Neptune.

The Greeks called the planets wanderers because they didn't understand the way they move. Actually the sun's family is very well behaved. All the planets move in a regular pattern.

The comparative sizes of the sun and planets and their distances apart cannot be shown in one picture. This is because the sun is so tremendously bigger than the planets, and the distances between the planets are so vast compared with their sizes. The relative sizes and distances are shown in separate pictures on page 19.

Rotation: 24 hours   Revolution: 1 year

The earth rotates on its axis once a day.
It revolves around the sun once a year.

The planets all move around the sun in the same direction.

How do the planets move? This motion is called *revolution,* and we say a planet *revolves* in its orbit — its path around the sun. In addition, the planets spin like tops. This motion is called rotation, and we say a planet *rotates* on its axis — an imaginary line through its center. Although we cannot actually see some of the planets rotate, there are convincing reasons to believe that they all rotate in the same direction as the earth does. (The planet Uranus is a special case, because it is "tipped over" so that its north pole points almost at the center of the sun.) The sun also rotates, but more slowly than most of the planets. It takes twenty-five days to turn once around.

Astronomers tell us that the orbits of all the planets lie almost in the same plane. To picture what this means, imagine that you are making a model of the solar system and you have a set of rigid hoops to represent the orbits of the planets. If you simply laid the hoops flat on a table, one inside the other, you would have a fairly accurate model of the paths of the planets. To make the model accurate you would have to tilt some of the hoops a little bit. But the remarkable fact is that the planets move so nearly in the same plane.

The distances between the planets are greater the farther they are from the sun. This increase in the distance from the orbit of each planet to the next one is regular for the four closest to the sun. But then between Mars and Jupiter the gap appears too big.

A German astronomer named Bode in the eighteenth century worked out a series of numbers representing the distances of the planets from the sun. He discovered that Jupiter, the fifth planet from the sun, was in the orbit where the sixth planet ought to be. There was no planet between Mars and Jupiter where the fifth planet ought to be, according to his figures.

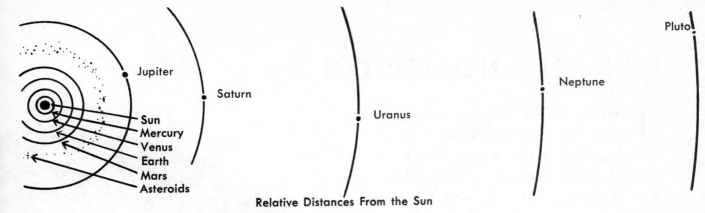

Relative Distances From the Sun

Bode was sure there must be another planet in that area.

How were the asteroids discovered? Finally, in 1801, a tiny body was discovered in orbit between Mars and Jupiter. It was named Ceres. Since then, more than 1,500 other tiny bodies have been discovered in this region. They are called asteroids. Ceres, the largest, is only 480 miles across. Many of them are a mile or less across.

Ever since the motion of the solar system has been understood, men have wondered how it all began.

How did the solar system begin? Obviously the sun and its planets must be closely related, since they all move together in such an orderly scheme. By studying the light from the sun and planets, astronomers have been able to tell pretty well what they are made of. They have not been able to detect any material anywhere in the solar system that is not also found on earth. In fact, one of the chemical elements, helium, the gas that is used in toy balloons, was discovered in the sun before it was found on earth.

Everything points to the fact that the sun and planets were created from the same stuff. Scientists figure there are two ways the solar system could have begun. The earlier theory holds that it began with a great cloud of whirling gases. The attraction of gravity drew the atoms of the gas closer together. As the gas condensed into a ball, the circular motion increased. Rings of matter were left spinning around the central mass. These condensed to form the planets and the central ball of gas became the sun.

The other main theory, which now seems more likely, is that a star either passed close to the sun or collided with it. This tore a great stream of material from the sun and sent it spinning around. Some of this material was moving too fast to fall back into the sun. It came together to form the planets.

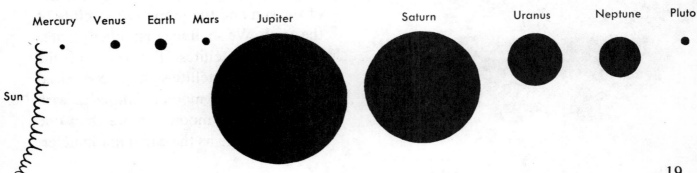

Relative Sizes

19

EARTH AND MOON

THE PLANET of most interest to us is our own earth. By a small margin, earth is the largest of the terrestrial planets, which makes it fifth in size of all the nine. The first thing an observer on another planet — say, Venus — would notice about the earth is its moon. In fact, from Venus, earth and moon would appear as two planets close together.

During the past few years, everyone has become familiar with the term satellite. The moon was the first satellite that men knew of. A satellite, as we all know since man has put his own satellites in the sky, is a body that orbits around a larger body. The planets are satellites of the sun and the moon is a satellite of the earth. We shall see that other planets also have satellites. But none of the planets has a satellite so large compared with itself as our moon is compared with the earth. The moon is more than one fourth as large as the earth in diameter.

What is a satellite?

The most important thing to remember

Why can we see only one side of the moon?

about the motion of the moon is that it rotates once on its axis as it revolves once about the earth. This is important because it means we see but one side of the moon from earth. It may not be immediately obvious why this is so, but you can demonstrate it to yourself easily enough. Take some object like a jar, with a label on one side, to represent the moon. Move it in a circle around another object — say, a milk bottle — so that the label is always facing the bottle. You will find that to keep the label of the jar facing the milk bottle you will have to rotate the jar slowly. This rotation will amount to one complete turn as your "moon"

makes one complete trip around the "earth." It is not just chance that has produced this neat coincidence between the moon's rotation and its revolution. The moon's rotation has been slowed to this speed by the pull of the earth's gravity on it.

The most noticeable thing about the moon as we see it from the earth is its apparently changing shape. From a thin crescent it grows thicker night after night until it becomes a full, round disk. Then it starts shrinking until it finally disappears entirely. The changes in its apparent shape are called phases of the moon. It takes 29½ days for the moon to go through all its phases — for example, from one full moon to the next. From this period come the months of our calendar.

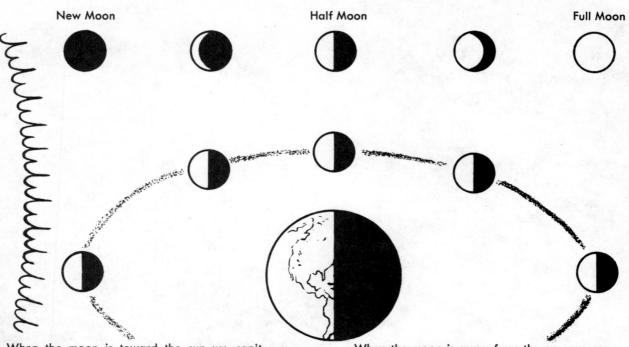

New Moon   Half Moon   Full Moon

When the moon is toward the sun we can't see it, because the lighted side is away from the earth.

When the moon is away from the sun, we see all the lighted side.

Of course, the moon doesn't really change shape during every month. It remains a globe. The light that seems to shine from the moon is the light of the sun shining on the moon's surface and reflected to us on earth. If you take a ball and shine a flashlight on it in a dim room, you will see that half the ball is lighted and half is dark. So it is with the moon — and, for that matter, all the planets as well. Half the moon is always in sunlight and half in the dark. We can see only the part of the moon that is in sunlight. And most of the time we can't see all of that half. The diagram shows how the different views we get of the moon make it appear to go through its different phases as it orbits around the earth.

Why does the moon "wax" and "wane"?

Notice in the drawing that half the earth is also always lighted by the sun.

Sunlight reflects from the earth to the moon just as it does from the moon to the earth. When the moon is a thin crescent, you can see faintly the dark part of it. It is "earthlight" — sunlight reflected from the earth — that lights the dark part of the moon. *Apollo* astronauts exploring the lunar surface were able to see the earth go through phases from "new earth" to "full earth."

Looking at the diagram of the moon's phases, you might wonder why, at the time of the new moon, it doesn't come between the earth and sun and cast its shadow on the earth. Similarly, it would seem that at full moon the earth would block the sun's rays from the moon. The reason this doesn't ordinarily happen is that the path of the moon around the earth is not in the same plane as the path of the earth around the sun. The moon is usually "above" or "below" a direct line from sun to earth.

22

ECLIPSES

What is an eclipse? But the moon must pass through the plane of the earth's orbit as it circles the earth. Therefore, the moon does occasionally cast its shadow on us. Similarly the earth sometimes casts its shadow on the moon. When this happens, it is called an eclipse. When the moon gets between us and the sun, it is a solar eclipse. When the earth gets between the sun and the moon, it is a lunar eclipse. When the shadow completely cuts off the sun's light, the eclipse is called total; when the shadow only partly hides the face of the sun, it is called a partial eclipse. A total solar eclipse is seen only by people who are in the area of the earth covered by the moon's shadow. This area is rarely more than 150 miles across at any moment and may be a mere point. But the shadow moves across the face of the earth as the moon moves and the earth rotates.

Astronomers sometimes have to travel to strange parts of the earth to

This is a solar eclipse, when the moon casts its shadow on earth.

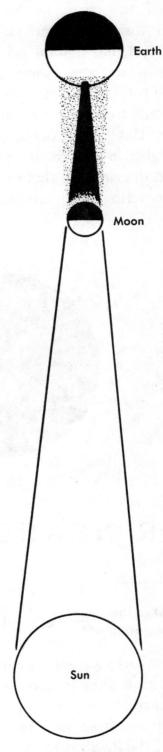

Earth

Moon

Sun

Solar Eclipse

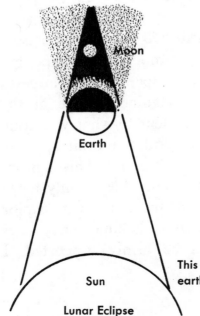

Moon

Earth

Sun

Lunar Eclipse

This is a lunar eclipse, when the earth casts its shadow on the moon.

watch an eclipse of the sun. The last total eclipse visible in the United States was in 1954. The moon's shadow touched the earth in Nebraska and moved through eastern Canada. On July 20, 1963, a total eclipse will be visible in northern Maine. At any one point a total eclipse lasts no more than about eight minutes and may be much shorter. But it is one of the most impressive sights in nature. Imagine the sun blotted out until all that can be seen is a shimmering halo around the black disk of the moon. Some of the brighter stars suddenly appear in the gloomy sky.

Lunar eclipses, when the shadow of the earth darkens the moon, are more frequent than eclipses of the sun. An average of about one total lunar eclipse a year has been visible somewhere in the United States during the past ten years. The moon doesn't quite disappear during such an eclipse because our atmosphere bends a little light around the earth so that the shadow falling on the moon is not quite black.

This is a total solar eclipse showing the "corona" around the blotted-out sun.

OUR NEAREST NEIGHBOR

Our nearest neighbor in space, the moon, appears to be made of rock, not much different from the rocky part of the earth. Indeed, it must have come from the same source as the earth. Some scientists think it was actually torn from the earth, leaving the basin of the Pacific Ocean.

What is the moon made of?

Since, on the average, it is less than 235,000 miles from the surface of the earth, we can make out some features of the moon's landscape, even without a telescope. With the largest telescopes, the magnified image of the moon is equivalent to what you could see with the unaided eyes at a distance of less than 200 miles. This is near enough to make out objects only a few hundred feet apart. You can go exploring on the moon with almost any telescope that can be firmly supported. Even field glasses show some of the major features.

Flights to the moon have provided a wealth of amazing information. The moonscape is now perhaps more familiar to some people than certain areas of the earth. But much of the data received has simply provided verification of "educated guesses" or observations and scientific conclusions prior to the lunar probes. We know, for example, that there is no air for men, plants or animals to draw upon; that the sun and stars shine at the same time by day; that the sky is black, not blue; and that the moon's gravity is a sixth of earth's.

What is the "Man in the Moon"? The moon's physical features have been known for centuries. Galileo was the first to train a telescope on it and see its landscape in detail, but centuries earlier men had named the major features that make up the pattern we see as "the man in the moon." These most noticeable features are broad dark areas, more or less circular. The earliest observers thought they were seas and gave them fanciful Latin names like the Sea of Serenity (*Mare Serenitatis*), Sea of Rains (*Mare Imbrium*) and Bay of

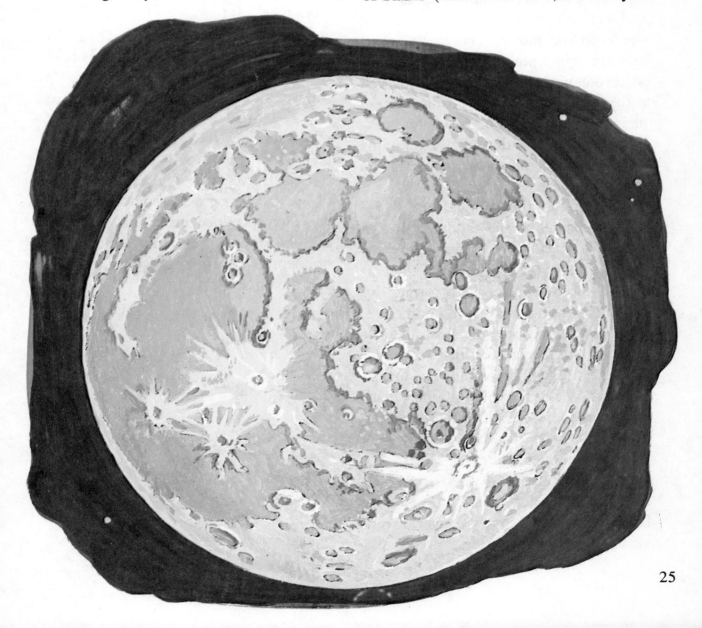

Crater on the moon

Rainbows *(Sinus Iridum)*. These dark blotches cover about half of the moon's surface. We now know there is no water on the moon. The areas called seas are broad plains, possibly of hardened volcanic lava and probably covered with dust and gravel. Around these plains the landscape of the moon is extremely rugged, with craggy mountains rising above the plains nearly as high as Mount Everest.

These mountains are made up of craters, which make the moon look like a giant's battlefield. There are two theories about the formation of the craters — one, that they were formed by meteors striking the moon; and, two, that they are extinct volcanoes. It may be that both forces have been at work.

There are also cracks in the surface called rills. These probably opened up as the moon cooled. And there are the mysterious rays. These are white streaks from some of the craters. They run across mountains and plains, in some cases as far as 1,500 miles. They may be dust scattered by whatever explosions produced the craters.

What causes the tides?

The moon has important effects on the earth. The chief of these is the tides of the oceans. Tides are caused by the pull of the moon and, to a lesser extent, of the sun. The moon pulls the earth out of shape as shown in the illustration. As the earth rotates, these bulges in the oceans move around the earth causing two high tides and two low tides every day at points on the shore. The pull of the moon, along with that of the sun, makes the earth wobble as it spins, which makes no end of complications in the calculations of astronomers.

Since we live on the earth, the study of the planet itself does not come under the science of astronomy. Because of the wealth of information available, its study is divided among a number of other sciences. However, the astronomer is concerned with the motions of the earth in space. These motions are of the greatest practical importance to us. They produce night and day, the seasons, and our calendar. Knowledge of them is necessary for time-keeping and navigation.

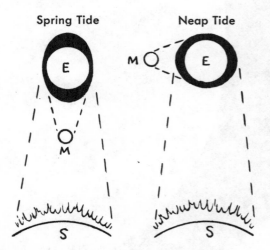

Spring Tide   Neap Tide

Tides are greater when the sun and moon are in a line, because the gravity of both acts together. These are spring tides. Smaller "neap" tides occur when the moon is at half phase.

DAYS AND SEASONS

What causes night and day?

"As different as night and day" is an old saying that illustrates how basic this daily change is to human life. Night and day are produced by the earth's rotation on its axis. We have said the the sun is always shining on half the earth, while the other half, away from the sun, is dark. Since the earth rotates, a point on it moves through the light and the dark every day. The rotation is from west to east. Therefore, New York moves into the light every day about four hours before San Francisco reaches the dividing line between dark and light.

Since the division between daylight and dark that you see in the drawing is a sharp line, you might suppose that dawn and dark would come instantly. That is exactly what does happen on a body like the moon which has no air. On earth the layer of air bends the sun's light and scatters it so that the sky remains light for a while after the sun goes down and grows light before the sun appears.

We tend to think of our twenty-four

The axis of the earth (red arrows) is tilted with reference to the plane of its orbit (yellow band). This causes unequal days and nights over most of the world.

hour day as being divided about equally between darkness and light, but this is true only for people who live on the equator. Elsewhere in the world a day may vary anywhere from six months to a few minutes of actual sunlight. This happens because the earth is tilted. Think of a plane, a flat sheet, running through the center of the earth and the center of the sun. You might suppose that the earth's axis would stick straight up and down through the plane, which would cut the earth in two at the equator. But it doesn't. The equator is tilted at an angle of 23½ degrees to the plane; the earth's axis leans over that much. As the earth revolves around the sun,

sometimes the North Pole is toward the sun, and sometimes the South Pole.

On page 29, you can see that when the North Pole is toward the sun, the circle of sunlight never touches the South Pole, and the other way around. Thus, days and nights in the Arctic and Antarctic are each six months long — half the time it takes the earth to go around the sun. In the Temperate Zone, where we live, we get day and night every twenty-four hours; but the length of time we are in the circle of light is longer or shorter, according to the season. We have long days in summer; short days in winter. At the equator, days and nights are each twelve hours.

28

The tilt of the earth's axis causes the seasons of the year. You can see below

Why do we have seasons?

that as the earth moves around the sun, one pole or the other is pointed more toward the sun. When the North Pole is toward the sun, we have summer north of the equator, and people living south of the equator have winter. When the South Pole is pointing toward the sun, it is summer south of the equator, and we have winter. At the beginning of spring and again at the beginning of fall, neither of the two poles is toward the sun.

The rays of the sun are more concentrated toward the center of the circle of sunlight on the earth. In summer we pass closer to the center of the circle of sunlight. We are also exposed to more sunlight each day in summer. This is because we pass through the circle of sunlight nearer its widest part. This is why summer is warmer than winter. The distance of the earth from the sun has nothing to do with the seasons. In fact, the earth is closer to the sun during our northern winter than in summer.

As the earth moves around the sun, one pole or the other is pointed more toward the sun, because the earth's axis is tilted. The slight change in distance from the earth to the sun during the year is not shown, because it has nothing to do with the seasons.

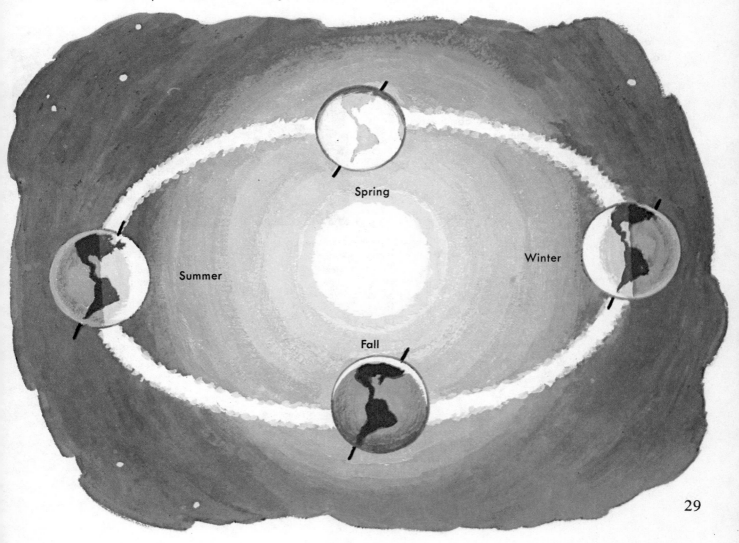

Spring

Summer

Winter

Fall

THE MAN FROM MARS

We know that other planets also have

**Is there life
on other planets?**

days and nights and seasons. One of the questions that has always proved fascinating to almost everybody is whether there are creatures on any of these other worlds to see these changes. The "man from Mars" has become one of the most popular subjects for jokes. Why Mars? We naturally expect that if life exists on other planets it would be on those most like the earth. These are Mars and Venus, the two planets nearest to us. Venus is toward the sun and Mars is in the other direction.

Of the two, the nearest planet Venus is more like the earth in size and distance from the sun, but Mars has been of more interest because its surface can be seen.

Mars was named for the god of war because of its red color, which is plain even to our unaided eyes. When Mars is closest to the earth and sunlight is reflected directly from it, a very modest telescope will enlarge it to the apparent size of the moon. Although we can't see its features as clearly as the moon's, we have been able to learn more about its surface than about any other object in the sky except the moon.

Viking spacecraft such as this one will land on the surface of Mars, while companion spacecraft orbit around the planet. Together, they will make measurements both in the atmosphere and on the surface. They will transmit information back to scientists on earth about biological, chemical and environmental factors. This will help us learn more about Mars and determine whether it could support life form.

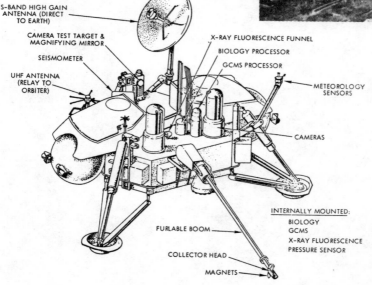

S-BAND HIGH GAIN ANTENNA (DIRECT TO EARTH)

CAMERA TEST TARGET & MAGNIFYING MIRROR

SEISMOMETER

UHF ANTENNA (RELAY TO ORBITER)

X-RAY FLUORESCENCE FUNNEL

BIOLOGY PROCESSOR

GCMS PROCESSOR

METEOROLOGY SENSORS

CAMERAS

INTERNALLY MOUNTED:
BIOLOGY
GCMS
X-RAY FLUORESCENCE
PRESSURE SENSOR

FURLABLE BOOM

COLLECTOR HEAD

MAGNETS

The most noticeable features of Mars

What are the effects of seasons on Mars?
as seen through a telescope are the ice caps at its north and south poles. These appear just as those

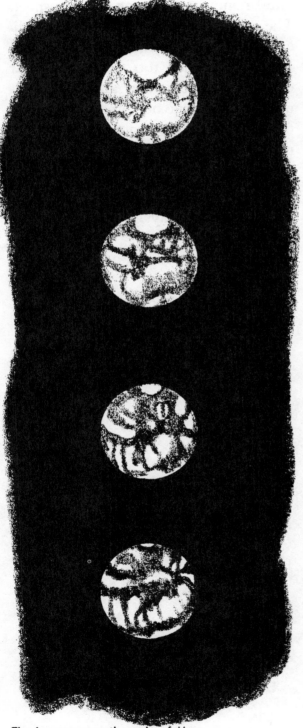

on earth would to a man on Mars. Since Mars is tilted at about the same angle that earth is, it has seasons as we do. The effect of the seasons can be clearly seen in the growing and shrinking of the polar ice caps. Another seasonal change has convinced most astronomers that there is some form of plant life in low-lying areas. These areas change from blue-green in summer to brown in winter. Seasonal changes also are accompanied by an effect that looks much as if water flowed into these areas of vegetation from the polar caps as they melt.

A great argument raged among scientists for many years about these markings. Some saw straight canals connecting "oases," from which they concluded that there must be intelligent creatures on Mars who had dug the canals to irrigate their lands. Astronomers at present are very doubtful about these canals, but they do agree that it appears as if moisture — perhaps in the form of vapor — comes down from the polar caps and seems to nourish plant life. They also agree that the lighter areas, which give Mars its red color, are deserts of rusty rocks. They have not been able to detect enough oxygen in the atmosphere to support animal life as we know it, but they do find evidence that both water and oxygen were once plentiful. The recent flight of *Mariner 9* spacecraft showed dry river beds on the Mars surface, possibly carved there during severe floods. It is quite possible that there once were creatures on Mars, and it is conceivable that they are still there, but it isn't very likely.

The ice cap over the pole of Mars shrinks and grows with the seasons.

THE MYSTERY OF VENUS

THE OTHER most earthlike planet, Venus, is wrapped in the mystery of its clouds. Its surface is effectively hidden from direct view, but it is presumed to be quite hot, dry, and dusty. Penetrations by radar, measured and analyzed, indicate that the landscape may be uneven or mountainous in certain areas.

Because clouds reflect light better than

Why is Venus so bright?

rocks, Venus is the brightest object in the sky aside from the sun and the moon. It can often be seen even in daylight; and at night it is sometimes bright enough to cast faint shadows on earth.

Venus was at one time considered to be a more likely home than Mars for earthlings, but revelations by way of space probes, radar, and radio astronomy are not encouraging in this respect. The average surface temperature is indicated at a rather uncomfortable 800° Fahrenheit! Then, too, there is no water on the surface; the atmosphere is deadly carbon dioxide; and the pressure of 294 pounds per square inch is tremendous.

The planet rotates in a direction opposite to its spin around the sun once every 243 earth-days.

Like the moon, Venus seems to change its shape, depending on its position relative to the sun and earth.

MERCURY AND PLUTO

BEYOND VENUS, toward the sun, Mercury orbits about 36,000,000 miles from the sun. No question has ever been raised about the possibility of life on Mercury. It has the most extreme conditions of any of the planets. Since Mercury makes three rotations for every two revolutions about the sun, its surface gets very hot on the side toward the sun — about 650° F. Its dark side is very cold, —260° F.

Mercury has no atmosphere because the gravity is so low. So there are no clouds and no rain on the planet. The surface of Mercury is probably much like the surface of the moon. Indeed, as the smallest planet, it is only about one third bigger in diameter than our moon.

What are conditions on Mercury?

Mercury is difficult to observe, because it is never very far above the horizon at night. Astronomers observe it in the daytime, using special screens.

The other planet that is classified as a "terrestrial" planet is Pluto, farthest from the sun. We know little about this planet, which was only discovered in 1930. Astronomers have figured out that it evidently has no atmosphere, and it may be made of black rock. It is bound to be extremely cold so far from the sun. Air would turn liquid.

THE GIANT PLANETS

To an astronomer just outside the solar system, all the planets we have described — Mercury, Venus, Earth, Mars and Pluto — would be insignificant. He would regard the system of planets as composed of mainly the four giants: Jupiter, Saturn, Uranus and Neptune. If he knew of the earthlike planets, he would probably think of them as minor fragments, much as we regard the asteroids.

With the curious exception of Pluto, the earthlike planets and the giants are neatly divided by the asteroid belt, three small planets huddled inside this band and the giants spread out beyond.

How big is the planet Jupiter?

Jupiter, the first planet beyond the asteroids, is the dominant planet of the whole system. Jupiter would hold more than a thousand earths. The earth is not as big compared to Jupiter as Jupiter is compared to the sun itself. Its diameter is more than one-tenth the sun's. But like the sun, Jupiter is not nearly so dense as the earth. Astronomers are fairly certain that Jupiter consists of a rocky core surrounded by deep layers of gases.

As befits the largest planet, Jupiter has the largest family of satellites. Thirteen moons have been discovered.

The clouds of Jupiter show changing patterns.

Saturn

These range in size from one as small as three miles in diameter to one larger than the planet Mercury! Jupiter and its satellites form a system comparable to the sun and its planets, except that Jupiter does not provide its own light. Far from it — Jupiter is bitter cold. Its surface temperature has been measured at 216 degrees below zero.

The other giant planets — Saturn, Uranus, and Neptune — are similar to Jupiter in make-up. Uranus and Neptune are less than half as big in diameter, but Saturn's diameter is more than three-quarters the size of Jupiter's. Saturn is the least dense of any of the planets. It is lighter than water.

What are the rings of Saturn? Saturn is the most spectacular planet of all to see through a telescope. This is because of its remarkable rings. These are bright, thin bands around the equator of the planet. The entire ring system is 171,000 miles across from the outer to the inner edge, but probably no more than ten miles thick. It has been determined that the rings are made up of separate tiny particles, each moving in its own orbit. They are probably ice particles averaging a tenth of an inch in diameter. In addition to its rings, Saturn has ten known satellites.

Uranus and Neptune are very similar to Jupiter, though much smaller. They also have satellites — Uranus five and Neptune two.

METEORS AND COMETS

THE PLANETS and their satellites do not complete the sun's family. There is an unknown number of smaller particles, possibly fragments left over from the formation of the solar system. These particles seem to move mostly in swarms with a few strays scattered about.

Meteors

The most frequent evidence we see of them is "shooting stars." These are fragments called **What are "shooting stars"?** meteors that are swept into the earth's atmosphere as we travel through space. They are moving so fast that friction with the air causes them to glow white hot, and they burn up, usually long before they near the earth, When a fragment does reach the earth, it is called a meteorite. A number of large meteorites have been known to strike the earth; one in Arizona produced a crater 4,000 feet across.

Some of these swarms of fragments have orbits that take them so **What are comets?** close to the sun at one point that the sun's energy breaks down the particles and drives gases and dust out behind them in a long glowing tail. These are called comets. Although they have in the past caused widespread panic on the rare occasions when big ones appeared, there is nothing to fear from them. The particles are so tiny and spread out that

Meteorite crater in Arizona. The meteorite apparently exploded when it landed.

the earth could go right through a comet without our knowing it. The paths of most comets are extremely long, flat ellipses, shaped something like a cigar. This means that it takes them a long time to revolve around the sun. The most famous comet, Halley's, shows up about every 76 years. It will be seen again in the year 1987.

All the bodies we have described — planets, asteroids, satellites of planets, meteors, and comets — make up the family of the sun. To us on earth this family is vast and impressive, but from the nearest star, the entire system is just a tiny speck among the countless specks of light in space.

Halley's comet

THE STARS

Our own sun is a star. Every one of the vast number of twinkling points of light in the sky is a gigantic atomic furnace, just as our sun is. And among the stars, our sun is not a particularly impressive example. It is about an average-size star, in between the giants and the dwarfs. (Giant and dwarf are not mere

What are the stars?

figures of speech; they are two classes of stars.) Of course, the sun's system of planets could not even be guessed at from the distance of the nearest stars. At least one of the stars we see as a point of light is itself big enough to contain our entire solar system!

How far away are the stars? The distances are hard to imagine.

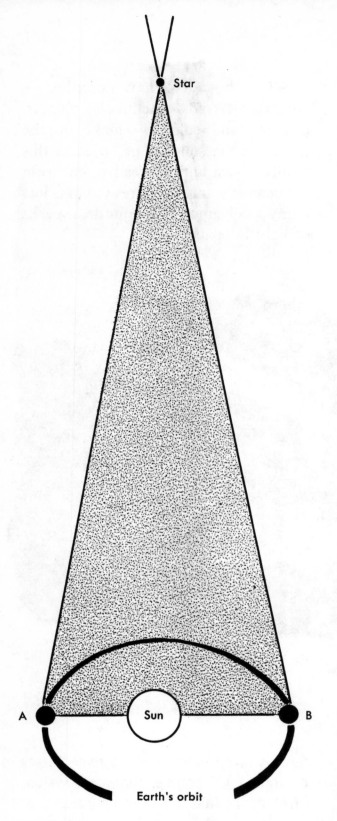

Astronomers measure the distance to a nearer star by observing it from opposite points in the earth's orbit around the sun. By noting the change in the star's apparent position from the two points, they can measure the angles of the triangle shown. Since they know the distance AB, they can calculate the distance to the star by geometry, a branch of mathematics.

The best way to deal with such distances is in terms of time, and that is what astronomers have done. You might say when asked how far you live from school: "About a fifteen-minute walk." Since the only way astronomers know the stars is from their light, they naturally use the speed of light to describe their distances. They say of a star that it is fifteen light-years away. Light moves at just over 186,000 miles per second. In one year it moves just under six trillion miles. Nobody can imagine six trillion miles, but everyone can think of the length of a year. When we look at the nearest star, the brightest star in the constellation Centaurus, we are looking back into time four years. If we should see it explode, we would be watching something that happened four years ago, the time it takes light to reach us from that star. Without using a telescope you can actually see back into time a million and a half years. The farthest light in the sky visible to the unaided eye is the Great Spiral in Andromeda, 1,500,000 light-years away.

At the beginning of the book, when we looked at the sky through the eyes of ancient men, we saw the stars as fixed to a sphere surrounding us. We noted that the brightest of them formed recognizable patterns. By now we know that both the celestial sphere and the constellations are only illusions.

We have seen that the lights of the sky actually come from bodies that vary in distance from a quarter of a million *miles* (the moon) to a million and a

How far away are the stars?

half *light-years* (the Andromeda Spiral). The second thing to note is that the stars that appear to form patterns usually are not close together at all; one may be ten times as far away as another in the same constellation.

Those stars that are brighter are not

Why are some stars brighter than others?

necessarily any bigger than the others. A star's brightness depends on three things: its size, its distance, and the kind of star it is. Some stars give off more light than others the same size. The brightest star in our sky, Sirius, is a small star that happens to be relatively close. The closest star is rather bright, but the next closest is invisible without a telescope. The stars were classified in ancient times by how bright they appeared. Ptolemy called this their magnitude. He broke the stars down into six groups, from the brightest (first magnitude) to the faintest (sixth magnitude). There are about 4,000 stars of the first six magnitudes. The term is still in use, but the measurement has been refined and extended until astronomers can speak of a magnitude of 21.3, for example.

One of the things that determines the apparent brightness of a star is the actual intensity of its light. If you watch a piece of iron being melted, you will notice that it first begins to glow a dull red, gradually grows more orange and then yellow and finally white. The colors of the stars indicate in much the same way how hot and, therefore, how bright they are. The red stars are the

coolest. The yellow stars, like our sun, are moderately hot in the scale, and the white and blue-white stars are the hottest.

These colors seem to be related also to the size of stars. The biggest stars are red, the stars in the middle range of size are yellow, and the smallest stars are white and blue-white. One of the most interesting things about this range in size is that there is not a tremendous difference in the actual amount of material in the different sizes of stars. The material is more spread out in the large stars and more condensed in the small ones. Ninety per cent of the stars we know about have a mass of not less than one tenth nor more than ten times that of our sun. The range of sizes, however, extends from dwarfs hardly larger than the earth to giants that would hold the entire solar system.

It seems as if the different sizes and colors of stars might represent different stages of development, and that is just what astronomers believe. However, they have not determined what the process is, since stars appear to fall into different groups when they are classified according to their various properties.

One theory is that stars are formed out

How are stars formed? of the clouds of atoms, mostly hydrogen, that are scattered through space. When enough atoms collect, the gravity between them pulls them closer and closer together until they begin to form a ball. As they continue to be squeezed together, they bump against each other so hard that they produce

more and more heat, until finally they start the atomic chain reaction that leads them to blaze like the sun. Finally, as it condenses more and more, the star becomes as compact and hot as the white dwarfs.

There is probably a limit to how far this process can go, since the more compressed the atoms are the more active they become from the heat that their collisions generate. Finally there is an explosion and the atoms are again scattered into clouds, from which the proccess can start all over again. Explosions have been seen that would appear to be just such an end to a star.

A nova, an exploding star.

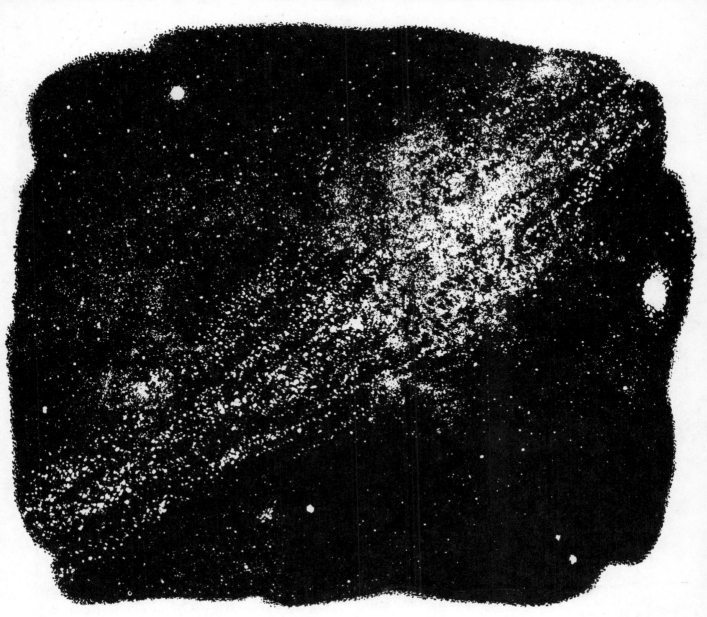

THE MILKY WAY

IN DESCRIBING the solar system, we noted that everything in it was in motion. With the improvement of measuring methods, men have discovered that the stars, which were always thought of as fixed, are also in motion. This real motion of the stars relative to each other should not be confused with the apparent motion due to the earth's rotation. The stars' real motion seems extremely slow to us because they are so far away. Actually, they are moving at tremendous speeds. And our sun is no exception. It appears to be heading at a terrific speed toward a point in the constellation Hercules, carrying all its planets along with it.

Where are the stars going? All those we can see as individual stars are moving round and round in one giant system called a galaxy.

From our position within this system we see the heart of it as a pale white band across our sky

What is the Milky Way?

— it is the familiar Milky Way. The Milky Way, as a telescope shows, is composed of stars so close together that they give the appearance of a shining cloud. This is an inside view of our galaxy. From far enough outside, it would look like a fiery pinwheel from one view and like a disk, swollen at the center, from an edgewise view. Our solar system is located well out near the edge of the disk. When we look at the Milky Way in the sky, we are looking toward the center of the disk; consequently, we see stars one behind the other, until they merge together. In a direction away from the Milky Way in the sky, we see only the stars in our own part of the disk, so they appear more widely scattered.

The number of stars in our galaxy has been estimated as high as 200,000,-000,000. It has been shown that the number would have to be more than 30,-000,000,000. The dimensions of the galaxy are somewhere between 100,-000 and 200,000 light-years across, and 10,000 to 20,000 light-years thick at the middle. Our sun is located 35,000 to 50,000 light-years from the center.

Two views of our Milky Way Galaxy from outside it.

+ is the position of our solar system in the Milky Way.

As we said, the whole system is in motion, with all the stars whirling around the center. Our sun would make one revolution around the center in about 250,000,000 years, and this is whirling, considering the distance!

When we look at the Milky Way on a clear, dark night, we notice that there seem to be breaks and holes in the light band. These are not holes, but black clouds of cold star material that black out the stars beyond. It is from this material that we believe new stars are eventually formed.

THE GALAXIES

What else is in the universe?

Is this galaxy of stars all there is in the universe? Far from it! We have learned that the Milky Way island is but one of countless galaxies like it. The nearest of these, the Great Spiral in Andromeda, can occasionally be seen by the unaided eye. It appears to be almost a twin of our own. In fact, much that we have learned of our own galaxy has been from observing it.

Not all galaxies have a spiral structure, however. Some seem to be formless. These are assumed to be galaxies in the making. Two of these smaller star clouds are very bright in the sky of the far Southern Hemisphere. They were first reported by the explorer Ma-gellan as he rounded South America on man's first trip around the world. Consequently, they are called Magellanic clouds. Other galaxies have a simpler elliptical shape than the spirals. They are assumed to be older and more stable systems. There are also some small "globular clusters" of stars just outside our galaxy.

Even the galaxies themselves seem to be grouped into systems. Beyond our group of about fifteen galaxies there appear to be other groups. One of these groups seems to contain over 1,000 galaxies. On a single photograph made with the 200-inch reflecting telescope at Mount Palomar, more than 10,000 galaxies were detected!

Having found that the planets move in a definite pattern and that the stars move in turn in a pattern in their galaxies, the question naturally arises: do the galaxies themselves move together in some stable pattern of their own? The answer is one of the most astonishing things that science has ever been faced with: the galaxies are apparently all flying away from each other at tremendous speeds and their speeds get greater the farther apart they are!

EXPLORING THE SOLAR SYSTEM

We now know a great deal about the

Why are scientists developing a large space telescope?

sun, the planets and the stars which make up our solar system. But we need to understand much more.

The oldest method for exploring space is the use of optical telescopes. They examine light reaching the telescope from other bodies in the solar system. But earth-based optical telescopes are limited by the earth's atmosphere. This is why NASA scientists are now developing a Large Space Telescope. Ten times· more powerful than the best earth-based telescope, it will be carried far beyond the earth's atmosphere by the *Space Shuttle,* a powerful rocket plane which can travel into space. Thus, it will be placed into orbit 300 miles above the earth's surface. Unhindered by the atmosphere, this telescope will be able to observe and accurately measure stellar objects.

Spacecraft such as *Pioneer* and *Mariner,* already proven in planetary exploration, will make further studies of Jupiter, Mercury, Venus and Saturn. New spacecraft, such as *Viking,* will land on Mars and study its surface, while *Helios* will investigate phenomena close to the sun.

LET'S GO STAR HUNTING

NOW THAT YOU know the "how" and "why" of the stars, you will want to know them by name. The obvious way to learn the constellations is by consulting a map of them. Charts of the major constellations are printed on the last page of the book. The simple instructions on the page facing this one show you how to mount the charts so that they will be most useful at any place and time.

When mounted, one side of the chart shows the sky as it appears looking north and the other side shows the stars to the south. The straight border of each cardboard mask represents the horizon.

The first thing necessary in learning to use the chart is, curiously enough, to put yourself back in history many centuries and imagine the universe as the ancients conceived it. Think of the sky as a hollow globe with the stars fixed to it and imagine that the globe revolves around the earth at its center.

Once we can picture the sky as a globe, we can fix positions on it by the same means that we describe positions on earth. Everyone has seen a globe map of the earth. If you look at one carefully, you will notice that there are circles drawn on its surface. Some of these° circles pass through both the North and South Poles. These are called meridians. The other circles cut the meridians at right angles and go around the earth parallel to each other. These are called parallels of latitude and the

one halfway between the poles is the equator. Both meridians and parallels are numbered so we can describe the location of any spot on earth by naming the meridian and the parallel that pass through it.

We can do the same thing in the sky. We can imagine circles on the celestial sphere that correspond exactly to the same circles on earth. On your chart the circles are parallels of latitude and the straight lines are meridians. The meridians appear as straight lines because the chart is drawn as if we were looking directly at the north and south poles of the sky. If you look straight down at the North Pole of a globe map of the earth, the meridians will look like straight lines running from the pole to the equator. The outer circle of your chart, then, represents the celestial equator.

Now that you have an idea of the "geography" of the sky, you are ready to put your chart to use.

When you set your chart for the date, it will show the sky as it appears about 9 P.M. (10 P.M. Daylight Time). If the hour is later, move it counterclockwise the distance of one meridian for each hour. If the time is earlier than 9 P.M., move it clockwise. This is necessary because the celestial sphere rotates. It turns completely around once every 24 hours. Therefore, in one hour it will have moved the distance between two adjoining meridians on the chart. This rotation is counterclockwise.

HOW TO MOUNT THE STAR CHARTS

1. You will need three pieces of heavy cardboard 7½ inches square. On one (cardboard A in the picture), draw a circle in the exact center, setting the compasses at 2¾ inches. Cut out this circle with a sharp blade, taking care not to damage the edge of either the circle or the remaining piece. Smooth the edges with light sandpaper, if necessary, to permit the circle to turn easily when replaced in its hole.

2. Label one of the other pieces of cardboard "North" (this is cardboard B in the picture), and the other "South" (cardboard C). In the center of each draw a circle 2½ inches in radius. Draw a line through the center and parallel to the sides of the cardboard. Now you must find the *latitude* of your home. It will determine the size of the cutouts in cardboards B and C. If you can't find it from a map, your local weather bureau can tell you the latitude of the town. Your latitude in the United States will lie somewhere between about 26 degrees and about 45 degrees. Now convert your latitude into inches for your chart by letting 10 degrees of latitude equal ¼ inch. Thus, if you live in New York City, which is about 41 degrees, your measurement will be just about 1 inch.

3. On cardboard B, labeled "North," measure off your latitude distance along the center line *down* from the center of the circle. At this point draw a line across the circle at right angles to the center line. Everything above this line within the circle is to be cut out, including the notch at the top, shown in the illustration.

4. On cardboard C, labeled "South," measure the same latitude distance *up* from the center of the circle, draw a line at right angles, and cut out the small portion shown above the line, as in the illustration.

5. *After* you have read all the instructions and know clearly how to put the chart together, cut out the star charts from the last page of the book. Paste one chart on each side of the disk cut from cardboard A, matching up the months exactly. With the disk in place in its hole, put the three pieces of cardboard together as shown, with the cutouts of B and C both at the top. Tape the edges together or glue the three pieces together at the edges. Make sure the circle turns easily. Label the horizon and celestial equator as shown. Instructions for using the chart are on page 45.

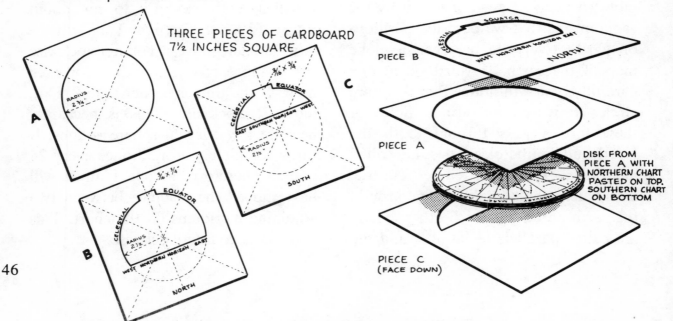

THREE PIECES OF CARDBOARD 7½ INCHES SQUARE

DISK FROM PIECE A WITH NORTHERN CHART PASTED ON TOP. SOUTHERN CHART ON BOTTOM

PIECE B

PIECE A

PIECE C (FACE DOWN)

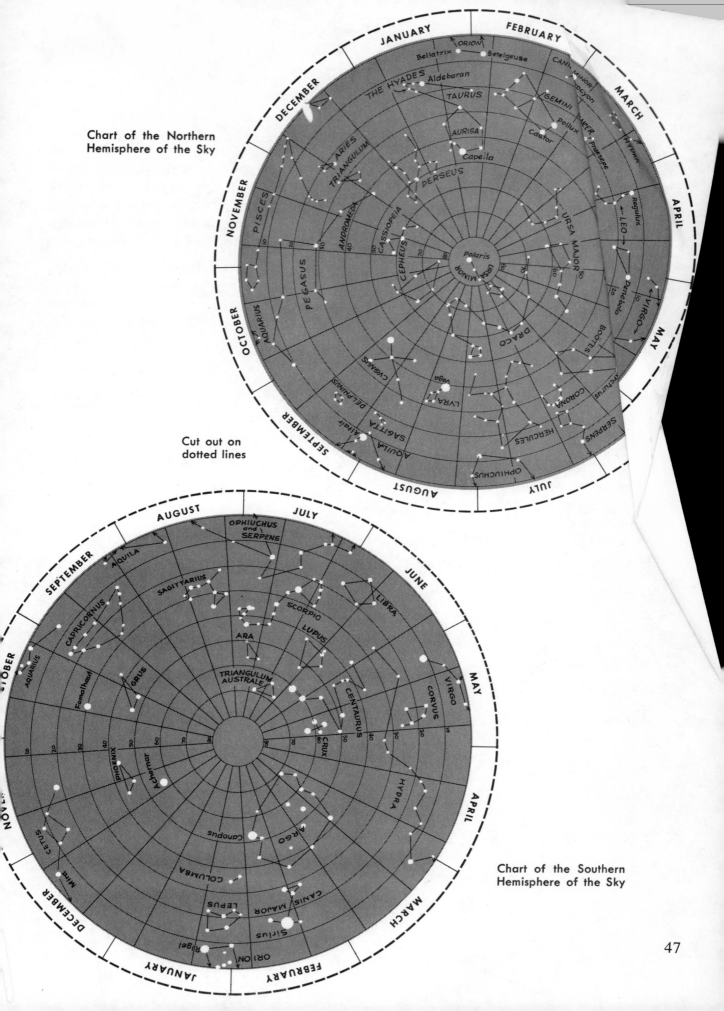

Chart of the Northern
Hemisphere of the Sky

Cut out on
dotted lines

Chart of the Southern
Hemisphere of the Sky

47